# BABE DIDRIKSON
## The World's Greatest Woman Athlete

# BABE
# DIDRIKSON

## The World's Greatest Woman Athlete

### Gene Schoor

Doubleday & Company, Inc.
Garden City, New York

*To Fran*

*As noble a champion in her own right*
*as the incomparable Babe Didrikson*

ISBN 0-385-13031-7 Trade
ISBN 0-385-13032-5 Prebound
Library of Congress Catalog Card Number 77–16944
Copyright © 1978 by Gene Schoor
All Rights Reserved
Printed in the United States of America

*BABE DIDRIKSON*
*The World's Greatest Woman Athlete*

# Chapter 1

IT WAS the evening before one of the biggest track events of the decade—the National AAU championships in Illinois, which would qualify the individual winners for the 1932 Olympics.

In her downtown Chicago hotel room, marking time for the biggest moment of her life, twenty-one-year-old Mildred "Babe" Didrikson was a bundle of nerves. She paced up and down the room. She bounced from one chair to another. She got down on the floor to practice the correct form for the start of her sprint and hurdle races. "Hands placed shoulder-width apart, thumb and fingers pressed into the floor, squat down on your toes." A dozen times Babe tried her starting position and then bounced up as an imaginary starter's gun barked.

Finally Mrs. Henry Wood, her chaperone and companion looked sternly across the room at the thin-faced young girl, now down on the floor practicing another exercise.

"Babe, you're as tight and nervous as a cat burglar, so stop your fidgeting or you'll wear us both out before the races begin tomorrow. Come on; let's go right out and buy you a new hat. A young girl needs a new hat, especially on her very first trip to Chicago."

"A new hat? Why shucks, I never had a hat before. Anyhow, I can't afford a new hat. I only have three dollars."

"I'll buy the hat," said Mrs. Wood. "It's my gift for you."

The Babe was thrilled. Here she was in Chicago for the first time, her first hat, and tomorrow the biggest day of her life—the National AAU track meet.

Mrs. Wood and Babe visited several millinery shops before Babe spotted a hat that she wanted—a pink felt hat with a cluster of tiny flowers.

"It's just the right hat for you, Babe," said Mrs. Wood.

"Gosh, it looks great," said Babe. "I'll never take it off."

Back at the hotel once more, Mrs. Wood ordered Babe to bed.

"It's late and we have a long drive to the stadium, so let's get some sleep—and take off your new hat, please."

But sleep did not come quickly that night. Babe Didrikson was too excited.

Mrs. Wood heard Babe tossing in her bed and moaning.

"Anything wrong, Babe?" she asked.

"I just can't fall asleep."

"Why don't you close your eyes and think of something pretty?" suggested Mrs. Wood. "Think of your hat, some nice young fellow back home. Just get your mind off the meet. You'll be asleep soon enough."

For a moment, the Babe lay still. Then she rolled and tossed about again.

"I've got these pains in my stomach," she said.

Mrs. Wood was out her bed, fast. She switched on the lights in the room.

"Where does it hurt?"

"Right here," said Babe, putting her hand down on where the pains were sharpest.

"Your right side!" said Mrs. Wood. "I'd better get a doctor!"

"No! No doctor!" pleaded the Babe.

But Mrs. Wood was already at the telephone.

"You'll need a doctor! It may be your appendix!"

The doctor was up in the room in no time. He was kind and patient as his fingers probed the sore spots.

"Does this hurt?" he asked.

"No," said the Babe.

"Does this hurt?" asked the doctor, his fingers moving.

The young girl shook her head.

"Well," said the doctor, gently covering the young girl with her blanket, "there's really nothing wrong with you that I can find."

"But I had these severe pains," protested the Babe.

"You don't have them now, do you?" asked the kind old gentleman.

The Babe shook her head.

"Not now."

"Just nerves," said the doctor.

He turned to Mrs. Wood, who was still pulling on her fingers in nervous anticipation.

"She's just excited," said the doctor. "The excitement is affecting the nerve center in her diaphragm."

"Thank you, doctor," said Mrs. Wood, considerably relieved.

"I could give her a sedative," suggested the doctor, "to quiet her down."

"No pills," said the Babe. "I've got that big meet tomorrow."

"You might take a lukewarm bath; that might help you relax," said the doctor.

Babe took the advice and soaked herself in a hot, sudsy bath. It did calm her nerves and settle her down, but it wasn't until almost morning, however, before either Babe or Mrs. Wood could fall asleep.

Neither could recall how long they slept, but it was a sound sleep and much longer than they had intended.

The Babe woke up first.

She looked around the strange room for just a moment before she realized where she was. Then, suddenly, she looked at her watch. It was late in the morning, perhaps too late for her to get to the track meet in Evanston in time for the first event.

"Mrs. Wood!" she called. "We're awful late!"

She was out of bed.

So was Mrs. Wood.

They rushed to get dressed.

"Just throw your track things in your bag!" said Mrs. Wood.

They hurried out of the hotel and into the street. There was a cab there, waiting in front of the hotel doors. They climbed into it.

"Dyche Stadium!" ordered Mrs. Wood.

"That's in Evanston," said the cabbie.

"We know it's in Evanston," said Mrs. Wood. "Hurry! We're late!"

"Relax, we're on our way," said the cabbie.

Traffic was heavy.

"Can't you hurry?" pleaded Mrs. Wood.

"Sorry," said the cabbie, "I'm going as fast as I can."

Mrs. Wood turned to the Babe.

"There won't be time for you to dress at the field," she

4

said. "You'd better dress right here. I'll hold this blanket up around you. Get into your track suit."

There was a crowd of athletes on the field, each club with ten or twelve or more contestants for the events of the afternoon.

Then the announcer roared, "Here is the one-woman track team from the Employers Casualty Insurance Company of Dallas. Babe Didrikson!"

Babe Didrikson, dressed in her natty blue-and-white track outfit, trotted to the center of the stadium, a broad smile on her face, waving enthusiastically to the crowd.

For just a split second there was a stunned surprise among the spectators as they watched the solitary representative from Texas move out into the sun. Then a wild cheer rose up from the stands. The sheer courage of a girl who single-handedly would compete for a post on the Olympics squad in competition with the finest teams in the nation got to the crowd like a shot of adrenalin. And they responded, as it always does to the man or the woman battling the impossible odds. The huge crowd thundered to its feet, roaring their support. They chanted her name continuously throughout that record-breaking afternoon.

"It brought out goose bumps all over me," said Babe Didrikson, speaking of her welcome at Dyche Stadium that afternoon. "I can feel the bumps now, just thinking about that unbelievable day."

The hometown support always seems to get the adrenalin flowing faster in the blood of an athlete and, for all purposes, the cheers at Evanston gave Babe Didrikson the feeling that she was performing before a hometown crowd. At

5

least that is the way she responded on that July afternoon in 1932.

She was like a Greek goddess, like someone possessed, as she moved from the 80-meter hurdles to the high jump, from the high jump to the 100-meter dash, from the 100-meter dash to the javelin throw.

She kept going. From the javelin throw she hurried to the 8-pound shot put. From the shot put she moved to the broad-jump pit. From the broad jump she dashed over to throw the discus. After she threw the discus she was ready for the baseball throw. It was almost impossible to keep up with her, but the Babe kept going as the cheers from the stands grew louder and louder.

She would stop briefly to change her shoes or take a swallow of water. Mrs. Wood would hand her a towel between the separate heats, and the Babe would quickly dry her face and hands. Mrs. Wood would give her a swallow of orange juice, and the Babe was off again for another heat of the hurdles, or the sprints, or the discus toss, the high jump, the broad jump. She was a human dynamo all over the field that afternoon.

There was good reason to cheer this incredible display of ability, for there never had been an exhibition of athletic prowess . . . courage . . . determination and all-around excellence to match Babe Didrikson's performance that sunny afternoon as she triumphed over one champion after another in almost every contest she entered.

Babe seemed to have mystical powers that day. Of the eight events she entered, the 100-yard dash was the only event in which she failed to score a single point. She had rarely performed in the shot put or the discus. On this incredible day, she defeated shot-put champion Rena Mac-

Donald with a toss of 39 feet, 6¼ inches. She placed fourth in the discus to gain one point. Next she won the baseball throw, with a throw of 272 feet, 2 inches, breaking her own record for the event. She captured first place in the running broad jump with a leap of 17 feet, 6 inches. She threw the javelin 139 feet, 3 inches, which bettered her own world record. She then ran her first heat in the 80-meter hurdles in 11.9 seconds, another world record.

In the high jump she was up against another outstanding competitor, Jean Shiley, a high-jump champion from Temple University. Both Jean Shiley and the Babe cleared the bar at 5 feet, 3⅛ inches. This was the record at the time, held by Fräulein M. Gisolf of the Netherlands. The bar was lifted another sixteenth of an inch. Jean Shiley cleared it. So did Babe Didrikson.

The bar was lifted once more, another sixteenth of an inch. The Babe couldn't make it. But neither could Jean Shiley. It was another first place for Babe Didrikson, a tie with Jean Shiley, but first place anyway.

The Babe had entered eight events. She won five of those events. She tied for first place in the high jump. In addition, she took fourth place in the discus and just missed scoring in the 100-meter dash as she placed fourth.

It was an unforgettable display. She had won six gold medals and broken four world records in the space of three hours in a single afternoon.

Perhaps even more remarkable was the fact that this slim young girl had piled up 30 points for her team, the Employers Casualty Insurance Company of Dallas. Babe Didrikson, of course, was the entire team.

The Illinois Women's Athletic Club of Chicago, with

twenty-two representatives on the field, was second with 22 points.

The Western Women's Club of San Francisco was third with 13 points.

The Meadowbrook Club of Philadelphia was fourth with 9 points.

"Babe, the twenty-one year old lass, who works as a clerk in the Employers Casualty Insurance Company at Dallas," wrote the reporter for the New York *Times*, "today single-handedly won the National Amateur Athletic Union's championship in track and field for her club and reserved for herself three places on the U.S. Olympic squad."

"It was a victory," he continued, "without equal in the history of sport and will rank for all time as one of the truly remarkable performances ever accomplished by a single performer."

George Kirksey, covering the events for the United Press, wrote of the Babe, "It was the most amazing series of performances ever accomplished by any individual, male or female, in track and field history."

Paul Gallico, sports editor of the New York *Daily News*, and later to become one of the best-selling authors of all time, said after witnessing her performance in Evanston, "I cannot think of any male athlete with the possible exception of Jim Thorpe who had come even close to spread-eagling a track meet all by himself, the way young Babe Didrikson did at the Dyche Stadium."

"You did it! You did it!" screamed a hysterically happy Mrs. Henry Wood as the Babe came off the field, tired and sweaty. "You won the meet all by yourself!"

"Let's celebrate," said the Babe, simply.

"You must be too tired," protested Mrs. Wood. "We'll just

get you back to the hotel. You'll just shower up and rest!" persisted Mrs. Wood.

"And then we'll celebrate," said young Babe Didrikson.

They did.

That night, some friends in Chicago took them out and they danced till three in the morning.

The next day, Babe loosened her muscles with a fast workout in Dyche Stadium.

"I don't want my muscles to tighten up," she explained to Mrs. Wood. "Besides, I've got to be in shape for all those foreign track stars. After all, I told my daddy when I was a small girl of ten that I would win the Olympic championship for the United States, and I've got to make good on that promise."

# Chapter 2

OLE DIDRIKSON's father was a carpenter but, like so many young people in Norway, where he was born, Ole took to the seas.

He sailed them all.

"I sailed around Cape Horn seventeen times," he was fond of telling his children. "I was only nine years old when I made my first voyage."

Cape Horn is at the southern tip of South America, Tierra del Fuego (Land of Fire) where the Atlantic and Pacific meet. The winds and tides are fierce around Cape Horn and the passage of a ship around the Cape most dangerous, but it was the only way to get from the eastern coast of the Americas to the western coast by water before the building of the Panama Canal.

"Once," Ole would tell his children, "the ship broke up in a storm and I had to hold onto a mast rope for hours to stay alive, to keep from being drowned."

"I held the rope with one hand," he said. "With the other, I held onto another sailor to keep him from going down."

There was another exciting story he often told Babe and the other children, about the time he and some of his shipmates were stranded on an island after being shipwrecked. The island was inhabited by a group of large monkeys, and being without food, the men captured several of the monkeys, killed them, and ate the meat. Ole never did explain just how he and his mates were rescued from that island.

"Some other sailing ship came by," was all he said.

Between voyages Ole had married Hannah Marie Olson back home in Norway. Hannah, the daughter of a shoemaker in Bergen, Norway, was considered a champion ice skater and skier. She had loved sports, even as a slip of a girl. When her father said he couldn't buy her skis, she made her own, out of barrel staves. Hannah was a natural-born athlete and was to pass on her prowess to Babe.

Hannah gave birth to three children: Dora, Esther Nancy, and Ole, Jr. Ole began to think of giving up the sea, settling down. He wasn't a carpenter by trade, but he knew he could make a good living at it. Actually, even at sea, Ole worked with wood, fashioning ships, enclosing them in bottles.

Once, a tanker on which he was sailing put in at Port Arthur, Texas, and he took a liking to the town. Perhaps it was the Gulf of Mexico that really charmed him.

In any case, on his return to Norway, he told Hannah that he had found a perfect spot for the family.

"It's a nice town," he said. "It's right on the water. Beautiful water. I'll get myself a job. Some kind of woodwork. And I won't go to sea any more."

Hannah Didrikson was delighted. It would be good to have her husband home, and she wouldn't have to worry about losing him at sea, as so many Norwegian women had lost their men at sea for so many years.

Port Arthur, Texas, became a dream in the Didrikson household. It meant a lot of stinting and saving to move the entire family, but they managed. In due course they all arrived safely in the Texas port town, Ole, Hannah, and the three children. Ole found himself a job as a furniture refinisher and, after a while, built himself a two-story house in the shape of a ship. The shape of the home was Ole's final gesture of homage to the sea he loved so much.

In Port Arthur, four more children arrived to liven up the Didrikson household. First there were the twins, Louis and Lillie. Then Babe was born on June 26, 1911. The last of the Didrikson children was Arthur, whom the family called "Bubba."

Babe was christened Mildred Ella, but the family called her Baby. It wasn't until she began school that the family began to call her Mildred.

"The 'Babe' came later," said Babe Didrikson, "when I began hitting home runs in baseball games."

When Babe was a little more than three years old, Ole moved his family some seventeen miles out of Port Arthur to Beaumont, Texas, after a savage hurricane struck Port Arthur. Winds up to 120 miles per hour and huge tidal waves ripped the town apart. The huge waves that poured through the Didrikson house swept away every stick of furniture, dishes, clothes. Six-year-old Lillie recalled the day: "We were so frightened. The new baby, Bubba, was born and we left the house. We didn't save a thing. We lost everything but the clothes on our backs. We just got out of town."

Beaumont became their new home. They rented houses for a time, until Ole bought a home on Doucette Avenue. It was a seedy part of town, and Doucette was a busy, noisy street with a trolley car line that ran down the center of the street. At one end of the street were railroad tracks, where the huge oil tankers rumbled constantly on their way to the northern markets. At the other end of Doucette was the Magnolia Refinery.

The refinery gave employment to many on Doucette Avenue. It owned the town's only radio station, and the Beaumont baseball and basketball clubs were financed by the refinery. You had to be rough and ready to earn your place at the refinery. It was a hard life. The street was full of rednecks and roughnecks, hard-working, rough-and-tough families living on the very edge of poverty, and Babe Didrikson growing up on Doucette Avenue had to be rough and tough in order to survive.

Ole Didrikson kept adding rooms to the two-bedroom house, until it was the biggest, roomiest house on the street.

Among other things Ole Didrikson built was a regular gymnasium, which he set up in the backyard. It included bars for high jumping and a weight-lifting device, which was kept in the garage. The whole family, Ole, Hannah, and all the children, were totally sports-minded.

They played baseball in the backyard. Every now and then one of the children would hit a ball into Hannah Didrikson's rose garden. Hannah loved that rose garden and threatened to stop the game.

The Didrikson children got around that threat.

"Here, Mamma," they called, "you hit the ball!"

Mamma wasn't about to get involved, but the kids were persuasive.

She picked up the bat and took a swing at the first pitch, and hit the ball right into her beloved rose garden.

There were no more threats about playing baseball in the backyard.

Football was a family sport, too. The boys didn't like playing with the girls very much. They had to stop tackling.

"Don't tackle the girls!" Mamma Didrikson warned.

So they played touch football instead.

A neighbor and friend whom they called "Aunt Minnie," an ex-circus aerial act performer, took them to the circus when it came to town. When the kids got home, they fashioned circus tights for themselves out of their underwear, hung a series of trapeze ropes in a chinaberry tree, and went to work.

They swung from trapeze to trapeze, fell on their backs, their legs, their heads, but, fortunately, suffered no broken bones. The chinaberry tree, which Mamma Didrikson had planted and cared for so lovingly in the backyard, however, was killed. All the kids got a whipping for that.

The Babe wasn't so lucky when she led her troupe in a game of follow-the-leader in the frame of a house someone was building in the neighborhood. The first time they played, Babe led her fellow playmates over the studs and the rafters to the top of the structure. From there, she jumped into the sandpile below, not knowing that there was a huge supply of lumber lying under the sand. The wood splintered and cut deeply into the side of her leg as Babe hit the sand. But a quick bandage and she was off again.

Undaunted, as she would always be, the next day she was back at the game. This time she really got hurt.

Nearing the top of the house, she missed her step.

"Watch out!" yelled her comrades in the game, but it was too late.

Down came the Babe. She landed with a bone-cracking thud on her side. She bruised and skinned her leg. Worse, she came home with three cracked ribs.

"I'd have gotten a licking for sure," said the Babe, "for coming home looking like such a mess. I guess the cracked ribs looked bad to Mamma. She didn't holler at all."

There is no doubt about it: The Babe was a tomboy from the moment she began to walk. She had to be to survive on Doucette Avenue, for the other boys and girls she grew up with were tough, hardy street kids, ready to fight at the drop of a hat, and the games they played got them in trouble more often than not.

On Halloween, Babe would be out on the street soaping the rails where the streetcar ran on Doucette Avenue. The streetcar would slide, and the motorman would have to slow down and stop—at which point Babe and her friends would jump on the back of the car and pull the trolley pole off its wire. The motorman would get off the car and fix the wire, while the kids jumped all over the car.

Once Babe got dressed in her brother Louis' old shirt and pants to pull the trolley wires. As luck would have it, Papa Ole was on that car. He saw Babe at the same moment that she pulled the wire. She began to run, slid in the mud, and almost went under the car. But she regained her balance and sped off home.

"Louis!" she called. "Papa saw me at the trolley!"

"So what?" asked Louis, indifferent to the danger that faced him.

The Babe made it clear.

"I'm wearing your clothes. Papa didn't see me. He saw your clothes!"

Louis was off like a shot. He crawled under the porch where his papa couldn't reach him.

"Where's Louis?" yelled Papa, in a rage.

"He isn't here," said the Babe.

"Wait till I get that boy!" threatened Papa; and Babe couldn't keep from telling Papa the truth.

"That wasn't Louis you saw, Papa," she said. "It was me. I was wearing Louis' clothes."

Papa Ole was stunned for a moment, and that moment was all that the Babe needed.

She was out of the door, out of the house, and under the porch before Papa Ole knew she was gone.

Babe stayed under that porch for a long time.

"You can come out," she said to her brother. "Papa knows it was me."

What saved Babe from the licking she expected, she never knew, but she suspected that it was because she told Ole the truth.

Another time, on the way home after buying some meat for the evening's dinner, the Babe stopped to watch a ball game in the schoolyard.

"Do you want to get into the game?" one of the kids yelled.

"Sure," said Babe, putting the package of meat on the ground. "I've got just a couple of minutes. Got to get this meat home for supper."

Those few minutes became hours, and suddenly there was Mamma Didrikson coming down the street, looking for her.

"I got the meat," yelled the Babe, moving out of the playground fast.

But someone was there before her, a stray dog, and it was finishing the last ounce of the Didriksons' supper.

"Mamma couldn't quite catch me," said Babe. "But she got hold of a piece of rope and whipped me with it all the way home."

"I was running as fast as I could," continued the Babe, "but Mamma could run fast, too."

It was all athletics for young Babe, racing the streetcar, hurdling hedges on the block, playing baseball with the boys because she played as well as they did. Of course, she had the usual household and other chores of children in a large family. There were the twenty-eight windows in the porch to wash, as well as the floors and woodwork.

"Get the dirt out of the corners," Mamma Didrikson would order.

There were after-school jobs to contribute a little money to the family and to put a little money into her own pocket.

She got herself a job in a fig-packing plant. The figs would come down a trough in acid water. Babe's job was to peel the bad spots off the figs as they came her way, clean them, and then toss them back in the trough. The acid made her hands quite sore.

She found another job, a job in a potato gunnysack factory. She sewed up the bags at a penny apiece, but she was fast and made as much as sixty-eight cents an hour.

"I'd keep a nickel or a dime for myself," she said, "and give the rest to Mamma."

Mamma Didrikson, incidentally, never spent that money on anything or anybody except Babe.

"Whenever I needed something," said Babe, "she would always have the money for me right there."

But work or play, Babe dreamed of the day when she would become a great sports star.

Papa Didrikson, himself a sports fan, would spend hours talking about great Olympic sport heroes. This was especially true during the 1928 Olympic Games, which were held in Amsterdam, Holland.

He would gather his children and read them all the latest results of the track events, the field events, then tell them stories about the great stars who won the gold medals and those who came close.

He told the children about the immortal Finnish runner

Paavo Nurmi, whose father died when Paavo was but ten years of age. So he was forced to leave school and go to work. Paavo did not have time to play games like the other boys, but he dreamed of being a great athlete, and he decided to become a champion runner. "Even as a boy," said Ole, "he began to train hard and to follow a strict program to develop speed and stamina."

Every day Paavo would race a suburban trolley car, mile after mile, to develop a steady, even pace. "This was not much fun," Ole said, "but Pavvo had his sight on the championship of the world, and he knew that the road to the top was not an easy one.

"He grew up to be a serious young man who did not speak too much. But he was ready for the 1920 Olympic Games. In his first Olympic race, Paavo was just beaten at the tape in the 5,000-meter run. But he came right back to win the 10,000-meter race and then break every record in the 10,000-meter cross-country race.

"That was just the beginning," said Ole. "Four years later, in the 1924 Olympics at Paris, Nurmi captured the gold medal in the 1,500-meter race and the 5,000-meter race in one day. The following day he won the 10,000-meter run and the 3,000-meter event to cap one of the greatest performances of any runner in history. And," said Ole excitedly, "I got to meet him and shake his hand." Seventeen-year-old Babe burst with excitement at the story. "Next year I'm going to be in the Olympics myself!" Papa Didrikson explained she would have to wait till 1932.

"The Olympic Games come only once every four years," he said. "Maybe then you can be in the Olympics."

"I'll be there!" announced the Babe.

It was a prophecy no one at home could really take

seriously at this time, but for the seventeen-year-old girl it was more than a promise; it was a goal she set for herself, and would make.

"Even before I was in my teens," said Babe Didrikson, "I knew exactly what I wanted to be when I grew up. My goal was to be the greatest athlete who ever lived."

"My dad," she added, "helped me to swing in that direction."

# Chapter 3

WHEN BABE DIDRIKSON was competing in the Olympics back in 1932, she was asked whether she was nervous or worried.

"Why should I be?" she responded in her always frank, open, and almost naïve manner. "I'm only running against girls."

The reporter, putting the questions to her, took a quick breath.

"How do you mean that?" he asked.

"I've competed against boys as long as I can remember," she replied. "If a girl wants to become an athlete and do some winning, that's what she has to do. Play against the boys. Get smashed around."

"You got smashed around?" queried the reporter.

"I've done some smashing on my own," responded young Babe Didrikson.

And she had.

Throughout her childhood and early teens, she was constantly in one fight or another.

"I dare you to step over this line!" she challenged, drawing a line in the playground dirt with her foot.

And she was at it again. It didn't matter whether her opponent was a boy or a girl—she took and she gave. Most often she gave a lot more than she took.

Once, when she was in high school in Beaumont, one of the school's football stars, Red Reynolds, stopped her in front of a crowd of kids.

"Tough, aren't you?" he challenged.

"Tough enough," came back the Babe, undaunted.

"Let's see how tough you are," dared the football man.

Babe put up her fists.

Red Reynolds laughed.

"I'm not going to fight you," he said. "I ain't fighting any girls."

"Scared?"

It was the Babe's turn to do the daring.

"I'm not scared," sneered Reynolds.

He pushed out his chin.

"Do you think you can hurt me?" he challenged.

The Babe just looked at him—or rather she just looked at that chin.

"Go ahead. Hit me!" challenged the football man once more.

The crowd of students took up the dare.

"Hit him, Babe! Hit him!"

"Go on!" urged young Red Reynolds.

"Go on!" urged the kids.

"Are you sure you want me to hit you?" asked the doubting Babe.

"Hit me!" demanded the football man.

And the Babe hit him.

She hit him just once, square on the chin, and down went Red Reynolds, down like a rock. The Babe, who was just about a shade over five feet tall, had knocked the hefty football player cold with a single smash on the chin.

"The only real first-class advice I can give on how girls

can be better athletes," she was to say once, in an interview with a sportswriter, "is get toughened up. But don't get too tough. There's a lot of difference there, between toughening up and getting tough."

There's a subtle distinction there, particularly when one recalls the toughening process of young Babe Didrikson as she moved through her childhood years, and her early schooling.

Raymond Alford was one of Babe Didrikson's special childhood pals. Alford was to become the local sports hero and eventually the "dynamic" director of Beaumont's school system. When they were youngsters, both Alford and the Babe lived in what was called the South End of Beaumont. It was on the poor side of the tracks.

"We went barefoot all the time," said Raymond Alford. "Some of us never did have shoes. Everyone was poor. We weren't collecting any relief checks, but we were poor.

"We used to play every sport known to man up in the trolley-barn lot. And Babe played with us all the time. As a matter of fact, she was the only girl who'd play with us.

"She didn't just hang around the trolley-barn lot. And she wasn't the last one picked when we chose up sides for a game. No, sir! She got picked right up there among the first ones."

They used to send her out to right field at first, when they were playing baseball. That is where they generally put the weakest players.

"She didn't stay there long," said Raymond Alford. "She was just too good."

Alford smiled, telling the story.

"Babe wanted to be the best," he said. "She wanted to beat us boys."

Raymond Alford became a bit thoughtful before he continued.

"I don't know now if it was because she was against men, or if she simply didn't like the idea of being feminine."

It's true that the Babe, as a teen-ager, never used makeup. She hated makeup. She never wore any kind of jewelry and never owned a pair of silk stockings, or a girdle, or even a bra. She wore sacky cotton dresses, socks that sagged around her ankles, and flat shoes.

Sportswriter Paul Gallico described Babe in 1932 in this portrait of Babe Didrikson, track champion:

"Her hair was shingled until it was as short as a boy's and she never bothered to comb it. She cared nothing about clothes and despised silk underwear as being sissy.

"She had a boy's body, slim, straight, careless, and she looked her best in a track suit.

"She was not at that time pretty. Her lips were thin and bloodless and she had a prominent Adam's apple.

"She had good, clear gray-green eyes. She looked, talked, acted more like a boy than a girl, but she was in every respect a wholesome, normal female.

"She was as tough as leather but she was one of the loveliest and most appealing characters of all the prominent girl athletes, and the easiest to understand.

"Beyond her ability in sports, she had no personal vanity. And nothing would please her more than to walk up to a rival and say, 'I'm going to lick you tomorrow.'"

And she did. Every time.

Some of these characteristics of the young Babe Didrikson would change with time, and she would wear stylish, expensive feminine clothes, jewelry, and even use cosmetics.

Babe started her school life well enough. She was a good

student and she got good grades. But one way or another, she never allowed schoolwork to interfere with her interest and participation in sports.

As a grade-school student at the Magnolia grade school in Beaumont, she would remain in the schoolyard where the junior high and high school girls came for basketball practice. And she pestered them to let her get into the game, which they did after a while.

Babe was good at basketball, even at that early age.

"You're all right," said one of the older girls as they watched her pump the ball into the basket. "Get a little height and you'll be playing right along with us."

The Babe grew up—that is, she grew older, in the natural course of events. But she was really a little girl, no more than five feet tall and weighed no more than eighty-five pounds, even when she got to high school.

At David Crockett Junior High, she made the basketball team. But in her first years at Beaumont High School, they said she was too small for the squad.

Ruby Gage—now Mrs. Bob Porter of Bakersfield, California—was Babe Didrikson's gym teacher in junior high. She remembers the Babe well and fondly.

She calls the Babe "Mildred," the name she was given at her christening.

"I never called her Babe," said Mrs. Porter. "I always had the feeling she wanted me to call her Mildred. I loved that girl.

"I remember her coming to school each day spotlessly clean. She wore skirts and blouses, mostly white blouses, but very clean and fresh. Her parents had trained her to be neat. I certainly can't imagine Mildred being a hippie. Never! I think she would have given the hippies a hard time.

"She was witty and in a teasing manner liked to catch the teachers off guard," continued Mrs. Porter. "She was wholesome, honest, bright, and a hard worker when it came to athletics.

"I loved that girl," repeated Mrs. Porter, the ex-gym teacher. "I loved her inner characteristics. I can only say good things about her. The other children loved her, too."

Lenora Branch—now Mrs. Edward Halfacre of China— recalled another side of Babe Didrikson's life at David Crockett Junior High School in Beaumont. Mrs. Halfacre was the Babe's home-room teacher.

She didn't call the Babe Mildred, at least not always.

"I remember the Babe coming into school one day," she says, "waving a couple of bills in her hand."

"I won it," said the Babe, as Mrs. Halfacre recalled the incident. "I beat a girl wrestling down on Buford Street!"

"She had some cuts and bruises to show for it," said Mrs. Halfacre, "but she also had two five-dollar bills in her hand."

Mrs. Halfacre mused a bit, then went on.

"The boys in my room," she said, "continually teased Mildred. They thumped her and hit her when she was going through the halls. But she had a way of getting even out on the school grounds. She would step on their heels. She would kick them. She never let the boys get away with anything."

Another teacher at David Crockett Junior High recalled Babe on the baseball diamond.

"I saw her pitch a few warmup innings for a men's baseball team. She was still in her early teens. It was really astonishing, watching her, seeing how natural her movements were. Her pitching motion, with loose arm and follow-through, were as fluid as those of any man on the field. There was nothing awkward about her."

But for all her natural prowess and skill, Babe couldn't make the basketball squad in her sophomore year at Beaumont High School.

"You're too small!"

Babe was keenly disappointed, of course, but she found some consolation in caddying at the golf course for one of the young physical-education instructors of the school, the buoyant Beatrice Lytle. And Beatrice Lytle proved to be a good pal for the youngster.

"I can still remember how her muscles flowed when she walked," Miss Lytle will tell anyone who asks, fondly. "She had a nerve-muscle co-ordination that is very, very rare. Not one of the twelve thousand girls I coached ever possessed the kind of co-ordination Babe showed me.

"She was the most teachable person I have ever known," she added. "You could explain the rudiments and the rules and she would go right out and play the game."

It was Miss Lytle who was the first to put a golf club into the hands of Babe. Golf was the game that Babe eventually chose as her favorite sport, and it was as a professional golfer that she went on to fame and fortune as the greatest woman golfer of all time.

"I'd let Babe use my clubs and caddie for me Saturdays at the municipal course," said Beatrice Lytle. "It was a horrible place, a pasture. There were lots of snakes, the greens were full of sand."

There are stories about the way Babe Didrikson smashed the ball 250 yards the first time she took a swing at it, but Miss Lytle waved them off.

"She could outdrive me after a few rounds," said Bea Lytle, "but that 250-yard story is a bit of an exaggeration."

Asked if she recalled the first swing the Babe took, Miss

Lytle replied, "No. I don't. All I know is that she didn't miss the ball. And that's not bad, is it?"

Golfing on Saturdays was fine for the Babe, but making the basketball team, at that time, was more important.

She went to see Lil Dimmitt, who was coaching the boys' team.

"Coach," she said, intruding on the man's busy schedule, "How about coaching me for a while?"

The coach looked down at the little girl. He was a kind and gentle man. Besides, he could read the earnestness in that little girl's gray-green eyes.

"Go ahead," he said; and he was impressed by what he saw.

"You want to watch the way the boys play the game," he said.

She did.

"Show me how to pivot," she asked.

The coach demonstrated, and the Babe practiced.

"How do you keep your dribble down low?"

"What's the best way to hold the ball when you're shooting a field goal?"

She plied the coach with question after question, and Coach Dimmitt was a patient and willing instructor.

"Tell those girls I can play basketball!" she demanded of the coach.

He smiled.

"You'll be playing basketball soon enough," he said. "Soon enough."

And she did.

In her junior year at the high school, and still no more than five feet tall, she made the varsity squad. They played her at forward and, from the very beginning, she became the star on a team that would go on to an undefeated season.

## BEAUMONT GIRL STARS IN BASKETBALL GAME

That was the sports headline, and the story on the sports pages was all about the stellar performance of Beaumont's new star, Babe Didrikson.

## BEAUMONT GIRL STARS AGAIN

That was the headline that followed the second game of the season and, again, it was all about Babe Didrikson.

It was that way right down through the last game. BEAUMONT GIRL STARS, and the star was the Babe.

In the newspaper polls she was named to both the All-City and All-State basketball squads.

She was undoubtedly the best player the Miss Royal Purples of Beaumont, as the team was called, ever produced on the basketball courts.

That junior year in Beaumont High School was a marvelous one for Babe Didrikson. It was also to prove a turning point in her life, in her career.

A great number of people were attracted to the Miss Royal Purples basketball games, primarily by the publicity it was getting because of the Babe's outstanding play. Among those people attracted to those games was a retired Army man, Colonel Melvorne (Mel) J. McCombs. It was Colonel McCombs who would move Babe Didrikson, and quickly, toward the ways and life of an Olympic Hall of Famer.

## Chapter 4

COLONEL MEL McCOMBS, a baldish, middle-aged, middle-sized man, was an executive in the Engineering Department of the Employers Casualty Insurance Company in Dallas, but his first love had always been athletics. He had played baseball, football, and had starred in track at Texas A&M and at the University of Missouri. In 1905 he returned to Dallas for a job with the Texas Pacific Railroad, and in his free time organized an athletic club, the Dallas Tigers. The Tigers played a good brand of semipro football, and in the summertime they turned to baseball. McCombs was the star quarterback, coach of the football team, as well as the star pitcher on the baseball team, but a trick knee ended his playing career.

In 1908 he volunteered and was accepted as the first football coach at Dallas High School. He also coached sandlot teams, clubs, and street-corner kids in all sports, often buying their uniforms and other needed equipment.

No one loved sports more than the colonel did.

"Boys and athletics make a proper combination," he said. He wasn't thinking of girls at that time.

Coaching was a hobby with him. He enjoyed it as much as the game itself, and maybe more. Any kind of sport, anywhere: If there were the kids to play it, McCombs was there to organize them.

He considered it a special stroke of good luck when the Employers Casualty Insurance Company of Dallas offered him the job as coach and co-ordinator of that Texas company's sports programs. He loved the job so much that he was on the job practically twenty-four hours a day.

With McCombs as their coach, the insurance company's teams became winners, and the Dallas office was suddenly alive with sports talk. Their teams were leading in almost every Industrial League sport, and the game became the topic of enthusiastic conversation among the young male employees in every section of the office.

The girls in the office were all excited about the victory string of the company's teams. But there was a rub.

"Why aren't there any girls' teams?"

A group of young women approached the colonel. They put the question to him.

"Will you help us organize a girls' basketball team, so we can compete in the Park Department League?" they asked. "And will you coach us?" they added.

Colonel McCombs had never coached a girl squad of any kind before. His entire experience had been with boys and young men. As a matter of fact, his experience with women anywhere was rather limited. He was what used to be called "a crusty old bachelor."

But he didn't turn the girls right down.

"I don't know," he said. "How do you coach girls?"

Then he answered his own question.

"I suppose you coach girls the way you coach boys," he said.

"That would be fine with us," responded the girls. "Just forget we're girls. Coach us like we were boys."

"I'm not sure," hesitated McCombs.

The girls pressed him for a positive decision.

"All right," said the colonel. "I'll try."

McCombs was a methodical worker. The first thing he did, after agreeing to organize a girls' basketball team, was to sit in on a couple of high school games. He didn't like what he saw. It wasn't the way the girls played the game that bothered him. It was their uniforms.

The girls were moving around the basketball court, running up and down the length of it, in baggy woolen bloomers, long stockings, and flapping middy blouses.

"This is a game that calls for speed and color," he said, collecting the girls in his office the next day. "You can't move quickly down the court in those floppy uniforms; we're going to add color and flash to this game. We're going to wear shorts like men's basketball teams—except we'll be more colorful, and I think we'll attract more people to the games, speed the entire tempo of girls' basketball."

The girls thought it was a great idea, but suggested that the uniform was something the entire Park League would have to agree on.

McCombs got to work on it. So did the whole town. Shorts for girls was a revolutionary idea at the time. There was a fiery controversy right at that moment on the issue in England, where the question of whether young ladies "playing tennis in Wimbledon in sawed-off pants that revealed a length of leg" split the sport columns. Dallas, in this respect, was no different from London. Editorials and letters, pro and con, monopolized the sports pages. If nothing else, the colonel had collected enough publicity for his girls so that their first appearance attracted as overflow crowd in the local high school gym.

Before the controversy, a crowd of 150 to 200 was considered a good attendance for the girls' games. By the middle of their second season, the girls' basketball team of Employers Casualty was playing before turn-away crowds of 5,000.

The first McCombs girls' basketball team wore a demure blue-and-white uniform. The second year they changed to orange and white. The third year their shorts were a bright orange satin. That's when the sportswriters started to call them the "Golden Cyclones."

It was for the Golden Cyclones that Colonel Mel J. McCombs recruited Babe Didrikson.

He had read about the Babe's incredible play, as the star of Beaumont High School's girls' basketball squad, in the local newspapers. One night he went to see Babe's team in a tournament game. He watched Babe dominate the game, flashing all over the court, scoring points from every angle. Babe scored 26 points in that game and led her team to the state championship that night.

Immediately after the game, Colonel McCombs approached Babe:

"How would you like to play on a big-time basketball team?" he asked the young girl, just fresh out of a shower and dressed, after the game.

The Babe's response was immediate and enthusiastic.

"Boy, would I! Where?"

"At the Employers Casualty Insurance Company in Dallas," said the colonel. "We play the leading girls' teams in the nation. We could use you on the team."

"What do I have to do?" asked Babe.

"I suppose you'll have to get your parents' permission," said McCombs.

"My dad's right here," said Babe. "Talk to him."

Papa Didrikson wasn't sure.

"Dallas is a long way from home," he said. "We'll have to talk with Mamma."

The colonel spoke with Mamma.

Mamma wasn't sure either, but Colonel McCombs was convincing.

Babe would have a job in the office of the insurance company, as a typist. She would be paid $75 a month—that was $900 a year (in 1930 a coal miner working eight hours per day received $725 a year). An ordinary office girl-typist got a salary of $675 a year.

Seventy-five dollars a month was big money for the Didrikson household in 1929.

Babe would leave school in February and return to take her graduation examinations in June. She was on her way.

She took an overnight sleeper from Beaumont to Dallas, some 275 miles by rail. She was wearing a blue dress with box pleats. It was a dress she had made at school and that had won her a prize for sewing at the Texas State Fair. She was wearing patent leather shoes, and socks. The hat she wore was the one she had bought for her junior high school graduation. She carried her entire fortune, the $3.49 change she got after buying her railroad ticket, in a black patent leather purse.

Papa Didrikson accompanied her on the journey.

In Dallas, Colonel McCombs met her at the railroad station. He had come down with the big, impressive yellow Cadillac he used to transport his basketball players. He drove Babe and her dad directly to the offices of the Employers Casualty Insurance Company, then asked Babe what work she liked best.

"I won a gold medal for the best speed on the typewriter," said Babe.

"Can you work a slide rule?" asked the colonel.

"No," said Babe. "But if it's numbers, I can learn quick."

That was the first job she got with the insurance company, using the slide rule.

The job settled, it was time to pick out a baseball uniform.

Babe looked through the uniforms. She looked for a No. 7. She had worn No. 7 in high school. She considered No. 7 her lucky number. She found a No. 7.

The pants were too big. She tucked them and made them fit skin tight. The shirt was too big. She took in the seams. Babe liked everything to fit snug tight on her.

"There wasn't an ounce of fat on me," she said.

Papa Didrikson helped her find a room. The rent was $5.00 a month. Then Papa took the train back to Beaumont.

Babe reported back to Colonel McCombs, as he had asked. He had plans for her. He wasn't one to waste any time. He wanted to test the young girl's ability with players who were more mature, had much more experience, than the high school girls. The Cyclones were playing the Sun Oil Company, the defending national champions, in a pre-tournament game. The game was scheduled the very night Babe Didrikson arrived in Dallas. That didn't matter to the colonel. He put her right into the starting lineup. He wanted to find out just how young Babe could fit into his all-star team. He had scouted her back in Beaumont, but that was a local high school game. Now he had to see if she could play with his all-stars.

The colonel had selected a number of other girls from Texas. These were also placed in secretarial or file-clerk jobs with the company. But primarily they were outstanding basketball stars. There was Belle Neisinger, a fine center from the little town of Grapeland; Lucy Stratton, an All-American, from Greenville; Marge Whitcomb, a big center, from Dallas; Mary Tate, a guard, was also from Dallas; Mary Carter, a fast-shooting forward, came from the little town of Hutchins; Ruby Mansfield, one of the greatest girl players of all time, came from Cisco.

Now, this night he wanted to test his newest player by putting her right into the important game against the Sun Oil team.

The national champions had a fast-moving team. They went after Babe right from the opening center jump. Babe doesn't remember how many reserve guards the Sun Oil team had, but she does recall how they kept crowding her, guarding her, doing anything to keep her from shooting for the basket.

"If one guard fouled out against me, there was always another one they'd send in," she said. And each new guard was tougher and rougher than the guard who had fouled out.

But the youngster from Beaumont fitted in with the all-star squad easily and was not to be intimidated. Her entire young life had been spent in scrapping and scrambling, fighting one or another opponent, boy and girl alike. She was all over the court, stealing the ball from the opponents and then dribbling down for a good shot at the basket. She was all over the court with an aggressive style of play that fired up the team and gave her instant recognition from McCombs.

"I broke away for my fair share of shots," said Babe. "We beat the Sun Oil team that first night by a pretty good score: 48–18."

Babe was high scorer for the game, with 14 points her first basketball game in the big time.

In the first of a number of unusual letters she wrote to her friend Tiny Scurlock, the sports editor of the Beaumont *Journal,* she said about that game:

"Dear Tiny: Played my first game last night the 18, and I never before practice with them and they say that I was the the girl thar thar they have been looking for. They put me to start and kept me in until the finish. Tiny I am a working girl and have got to get busy. Please keep this write up [she had enclosed a press clipping on the game] or send it back when you get a chance. Thanks so much, Babe."

Two days later she wrote another note to Tiny:

"Dear Tiny: The games are coming in pretty fast here lately. We played Seagoville again last night and tomorrow at Cisco, Texas, and Monday night we play the champs of city. They have beaten the Cyclones but if I can help it they wont do it anymore. I am sending two write ups & me box score. they don't give you any write ups here. Well Good by Babe P.S. Please save write up for me."

Babe Didrikson was a happy young girl. She knew now that her dream of becoming an outstanding sports star was no longer a dream. She was on her way.

# Chapter 5

BABE DIDRIKSON hadn't been playing more than a month before she began to receive offers from around the basketball circuit, offers from other companies trying to lure her away from Employers Casualty. On March 6, 1930, she wrote to Tiny:

"Dear Tiny: Boy I am still knocking them cold, we started in the S.A.A.U. [Southern Amateur Athletic Union] tournament this week and are still holding out very fine and hope we keep on. We played the Western Union Tuesday night and beat them 62 to 9 and we played the Evary team last night and we beat them 82 to 5 [an enclosed box score showed Didrikson with 36 points in this game]. We have two All American guards and two All American forwards on our team and Mr. McCombs said that he would have three All American Forwards and Three All American Guards before the season is over. So Tiny I am up here now and that is what I am going to be, just watch and see. I will be home I guess about April the 3rd or the 5th somewheres around there, that is after the National A.A.U. is over and I get that All American Badge to put on my left sleeve of this hot orange sweater that I have. "Tiny"—I have had two more offers and they are from the Sun Oil and the Sparkman of Ark. The Oil Man said that he could use me in the national this year but I am going to stay with the Golden Cyclones until this season is over, we have a new coach and our playing is 100% better. "Tiny" How was the picture and what have you done with it, maybe in the nationals I will be able to send to Beaumont a picture of me in the news paper about the national A.A.U. Hope so anyhow. Well to be frank with you I am going to make All American cause I have got my mind set on that. Well Tiny I have to close. Good by. Babe."

There was no letup in the new job offers as the season progressed. The Kansas City Life Insurance Company offered her not only a raise in salary, as did several other companies around the country, but they threw in a lot of other inducements as well.

Babe could have any kind of job she wanted with the Kansas-based insurance company.

"If you have had no experience do not hesitate to say so as that will have no bearing on your opportunity," they wrote her.

They threw in free medical attention.

They threw in a sliding scale of bonuses for every win.

The Golden Cyclones in 1930—the year that saw Babe Didrikson's debut in big-time basketball—lost the national championship to the Sunoco Oilers at Wichita, Kansas, by just a point. Babe scored 210 points in the five tournament games, attracted tremendous attention, and when the finals had been played, she was selected by the sportswriters at the game as an All-American forward.

It was a remarkable year for the young girl, who still had to go back to Beaumont to get her high school diploma. And the extra pay and all the benefits that came with that promise were very tempting to the youngster, who was tasting national publicity for the first time in her young life.

Employers Casualty did not increase her salary, but they were doing something that was more important for Babe Didrikson at the moment: Colonel Mel McCombs was organizing a girls' track and field squad, and the prospect of running, hurdling, and throwing the javelin was too exciting, too challenging for Babe to consider a change of jobs.

She stayed with the Employers Casualty Insurance Company, living in a $5.00-a-month room on Haines Street, Dallas, in the Oak Cliff section of the city. It was a quiet, tree-lined street, where she lived with the rest of the Golden Cyclones. She had her breakfast, with all the other girls, at Danny Williams' house. Danny Williams was the assistant coach for the Golden Cyclones, and his wife was a good cook.

"I can still remember her pies with graham cracker crust," the Babe would say.

It was $.15 for breakfast. It was $.35 for dinner at Danny Williams' table.

For lunch, it was always toasted cupcakes and a Coke in the nearby drugstore.

Prices for food in those days, of course, were considerably lower than prices today, when a sandwich and a Coke cost more than a dollar. Babe got along very well on her salary of $75, of which $45 went regularly back to her mother and father in Beaumont.

Colonel McCombs helped out a bit. He would drive his star basketball forward to work, and back home again after work, so that she could save the carfare.

The colonel had been thinking of organizing a girls' track team for some time. It was probably because he wanted to get the girls' reaction to his idea that he took Babe to a track meet at Lakeside Park, in Dallas, one Saturday afternoon.

Babe had read about track meets before, and she had listened excitedly as her father had related the track heroics at the 1928 Olympics. But she had never seen a live track meet.

At Lakeside Park, her heart beat faster and her pulse quickened as she watched the runners, the hurdlers. It brought back memories of her hedge-jumping in Beaumont. She recalled her girlhood ambitions. She remembered the promise she had made her father.

"I'm going to be in the next Olympics, in 1932!"

There was a long stick lying on the ground.

She picked it up.

"What's this?" she asked the colonel. The stick was heavier than she had thought it would be.

"It's a javelin," said the colonel. "You throw it like a spear."

"I know you throw it like a spear," said Babe. "I just didn't know what it looked like."

She picked up the javelin and hurled it, like someone who had been hurling javelin for years.

The javelin traveled. It traveled a good distance.

"Pretty good," said Colonel McCombs.

"I can do better than that," said Babe Didrikson.

And, eventually, she certainly did.

There was no doubt in her mind about her ability to make the girls' track team at Employers Casualty. The other girls in the office were just about as enthusiastic as Babe was. McCombs organized the girls' track team for the insurance company, and it was to make track history—at least, one member of that track team was to make history: Babe Didrikson.

Anything Babe undertook to do, she worked hard at. She had to be No. 1 in whatever she did.

There was the regular two to three hours of practice every afternoon. But that wasn't enough. After dinner, she was in her tennis shoes, sprinting up the hill on Haines Street to develop endurance, practicing various exercises to strengthen her arms and legs. Then it was out to Lakeside Park, where she would run and jump and hurdle until it got dark.

She practiced timing her spring for the broad jump. She practiced leaping high into the air for the high jump. She had been told to pace herself in the 440-yard run, but she practiced by sprinting the 440-yard dash, and she outran everyone else.

She wrote another letter to Tiny on May 21, 1930:

"Dearest Tiny—Have been very busy with track, and track meet that we had Saturday against S.M.U. [Southern Methodist University]. Our team won plenty easy with about 48 points to the good. The reason why I haven't written to you is because I have had nothing to say, we have been out every evening for track practice and are going out again. I am the track captain, we elected right after the meet at S.M.U. Saturday. I am enclosing the write ups that they gave us in the paper. So that you can see how everything came out. Next Sunday Kate Carriager and myself are going to practice for Tennis doubles and gonna take everything. We have played base ball three times and won all three games, we played Davis Hat Company yesterday and beat them 26 to 4, easy game. Boy Tiny if I hadn't sat down on that last broad jump I could have broken the world's record just like taking candy from a baby. But next Saturday the 31th and I am gonna break a record in every thing that I go out for.

Last Saturday I entered four things and won first in all four. In about three or four days Jacoby will give us our medals. That is four to the string that I am heading for. Well, by and get that thing ready so that I can see it [referring to the contract between them], I don't think so much about that letter [the Kansas City offer] do you? Until next time. Babe Didrikson."

In the very first meet against Southern Methodist University, Babe Didrikson was entered in four events. She won gold medals in the broad jump, the high jump, the 100-yard dash, and the 440-yard dash.

On June 8, 1930, in another of her notes to Tiny, she wrote: "Dear Tiny—Just got back from Shreveport from the Southern Track meet. Well that makes the 13th gold medal that I have gotten. Made me a bracelet out of the first ten that I got and I got 3 from the Southern Meet. All gold and no silver. I am sending you a write up from the Times.

"Why don't you drop me a line once in a while and tell me about what you are going to do. Well Tiny I have got to go out to the track field at S.M.U. and brush up for the Texas and the National meet. So that I can Break a few worlds records.

"I am going to enter the tennis, swimming and every other kind of meet over here and over there, get full of medals. You know like ants.

"Some typest Huh? Just Babe. Babe."

Three days before her birthday (June 28, 1930), she scrawled a quick note: "Dear Tiny. Had the Texas A.A.U. Track Meet Saturday. We have had 4 track meets so far, and Tiny I have made first place in all four of them and have

March 1930. One month after leaving her hometown of Beaumont,
Texas, to play basketball with the Golden Cyclones team of Dallas,
Babe Didrikson wrote her friend, sports editor Tiny Scurlock at the
Beaumont *Journal,* "Dear Tiny. We beat every team in the national
AAU championship, but lost in the finals to Sun Oil by 1 point. I was
lucky. . . scored 210 points in the five games and everybody is talking
about yours truly."

1931 national AAU champs. The Golden Cyclones basketball team won the national AAU championship in 1931, led by Babe Didrikson, who scored 195 points in six games. Left to right, team members are: Lalia Warren, Ruby Mansfield, Pat Meith, Babe Didrikson, Belle Neisinger, Lucy Stratton, Agnes Lori, Kathleen Peace.

Babe Didrikson wins national AAU meet single-handedly. Here is a closeup of nineteen-year-old Babe Didrikson just prior to the start of the 1932 national AAU track and field championships at Evanston, Illinois, on July 16. Babe set the entire track world and the nation on fire as she captured first place in five events, tied for first in another event, and set a new world record for the javelin throw. She captured first place in the 80-meter hurdles, tied for first in the high jump, won the baseball throw, the shot put, and the broad jump, and outclassed the field in the javelin throw.

(Photo Courtesy Employers Casualty Insurance Company, Dallas)

In the Olympic Games of 1932 held in Los Angeles, Babe Didrikson won gold medals in the 80-meter hurdles and the javelin throw. Here she poses to show the marvelous form that won her the Olympic championship with the javelin.

1932 Olympics in Los Angeles, Babe Didrikson lost the gold medal in the high jump when the judges ruled that her dive (shown) over the bar was illegal. Her rival, Jean Shiley, was declared the winner of the gold medal, while the Babe had to be content with the silver medal. However, both girls were named as coholders of the world record for the jump, as both girls cleared 5 feet, 5¼ inches.

(Photo Courtesy Dallas *Morning News* Sports Department)

But Babe won her share of medals at the Olympics. Here she is on the victory stand, with archrival Evelyne Hall at the left.

(Photo Courtesy Dallas *Morning News* Sports Department)

Two great stars meet. Babe Didrikson shows the Philadelphia Athletics' great home-run slugger Jimmy Foxx how she holds the ball for a curve. The pair of champions were photographed together at Fort Meyers, Florida, on March 20, 1934, when the Babe pitched one inning for the Athletics against the Brooklyn Dodgers.

Babe pitches to the Dodgers. Babe Didrikson was a very good baseball player. In the photo she is shown pitching against the Brooklyn Dodgers in an exhibition game during 1934 spring training. The Babe pitched one inning for the Philadelphia Athletics.

ᵃ
ʰᵃᵛ been high pointer in all. I have a record in every meet and everything that I have. Boy! I surely did cut my foot. I was just going out for practice Thursday and the bathhouse had a broken bottle all over the floor and of course I would step on the biggest piece. I went to the Doctor 2 times and he gouged around and made it so sore, but boy did i jump. And throw that Ball & Javelin, put the shot. Just read these write ups and see. High Jump ½ inch below the World record. My team has won all the meets so far. The National meet will be a fight between Chicago and Cyclones of Dallas. Mr. McCombs has us guessed winning by six points. Mighty good guesser, has guessed every meet and wasn't 1 point less on all but one and perfect on it—70 and our score was 70. Well Tiny how about a nice write up over there in Beaumont, remember the scrape book is almost full. Oh! yeah! Right after the Track season I am gonna train for the Olympics in 1932 on the Broad Jump, High Jump true Western roll, Baseball and Javelin Throw. Train 5 times a week into 1932. Practice makes perfect. Boy at the National & Olympic gonna show everyone I have ants in my pants. By—Babe— P.S. Please send these write ups to my mamma, have gotten 18 gold medals and no silver or bronze. Thanks—Babe. And the rest you have of me put them in my scrape book. Babe."

She swam with the swimming team for Employers Casualty, and she was a fine diver. She was the star pitcher for the baseball team, and played third base when she wasn't pitching. But track was the most important thing.

Another note to Tiny on July 8: "Dear Tiny! Here is where I ought to get a big write up in the Beaumont. Tiny I was one of six girls from America to go to Germany next August 1930 and Tiny Mr. Bingham President of the National A.A.U. and all of the officials said that I had a berth on the

Olympic team in the 1932 without a doubt. Tiny fix me up a good write up. I will send you a brief scetch. I have broken 6 American records, 7 or 8 Southern records and 4 world records. I broke three word records in the national the 4th [of July]. I broke the Javelin which was 129 feet and I threw it 133 6½ inches. New world record official baseball which was 258 feet I broke it by 268 feet. And broke it in an exhibition 274 feet and Tiny you know Stella Walsh . . . beat me in the broad jump. We both broke the world's record. My first jump I fouled. I jumped 18 feet 11½ inches, but the foul didn't count. My second jump was 18 feet 8¾ in and hers was 18 feet 9⅛ inches. Tough luck. The old world record is 18 feet 7½ inches. Well Tiny I get a vacation pretty soon and I guess I will come home for about 4 or 5 days. And then I will tell you about the trip to Germany. Yours for a big headline. Babe."

The trip to Germany did not materialize, but the Golden Cyclones finished second in the 1930 AAU track meet, as Babe broke all records in the javelin, the baseball throw, and the 80-meter dash.

In the 1931 basketball season, Babe was All-American again, scoring 195 points in six games, and in the championship game the Golden Cyclones defeated Wallenstein-Raffman of Wichita, 34–32.

The insurance company management began to worry about the offers Babe Didrikson was getting to lure her out of Dallas. They did nothing about raising her salary, but in a number of ways the company tried to show their affection. The president of the company began to personally drive the Babe to the Dallas Country Club, and paid for her golf lessons.

Babe wasn't taken in by this "friendly" and "generous"

treatment. She knew what she was worth to the company, for all the national publicity she was getting, both for Employers and herself, and she was beginning to be annoyed about the situation. She was also under constant pressure from home to send all the money she could manage, Ruth Scurlock, Tiny Scurlock's wife, recalled. "Babe's family was really in poor financial shape, and they always had their hand out to her—she never had much money because she freely handed out regular sums to the family."

There was also a new and perplexing situation that the Babe had to contend with in the insurance company's offices. She was getting tremendous national publicity, as she well deserved, but her teammates and colleagues began to resent the attention and the favoritism shown by the press and her employer.

"At first," said one of her teammates, "we were very proud of her. She was modest and likable, and we were all very friendly—at first. But then, with all the people and the papers making all that fuss about her, she became quite cocky. We didn't like that at all."

People did make a fuss about her.

At the AAU meet in Jersey City Babe was the individual star of the meet. She won the baseball throw, the 80-meter hurdle, and the broad jump, scoring 15 points for the Golden Cyclones. And as the meet ended, the mounted police had to clear the field when the crowd poured out of the stands in their hungry attempt to reach out to touch the great young athlete.

"She was a great athlete," said another of Babe's teammates, "but she bragged so much that it made us mad."

Babe Didrikson was a cocky young girl. There was no doubt about that, but the cockiness was no more than a display of the confidence she had in her own ability. An athlete cannot be a winner without that kind of confidence.

Her "bragging," too, was more than a display of confidence. It was an expression of the joy she found in winning.

Still, the reaction of the teammates around her—whether it was justified or just plain jealousy—didn't make Babe Didrikson particularly happy or comfortable.

She became petulant.

"These girls here are just like they were in Beaumont High School. Jealous," she wrote to her friend Tiny Scurlock back home. It was the first time she had ever said anything about the jealousy of her schoolmates.

"They're all trying to beat me and they can't," she continued in her letter.

And this was the simple truth.

"Tiny," she went on, "if I get another letter from Wichita, I'm going to take their offer."

She got more than one offer from Wichita, and from all over the country, but despite continuous differences and arguments she was to remain loyal to her Dallas team, and she performed brilliantly during the 1932 basketball season. Her team was the runner-up in the national championship for the second time, and she was once again named to the All-American team.

The strained relationship among the girls of the Golden Cyclones eased up. The girls were all speaking to each other again, friends once again. Babe did continue to think that she ought to be getting a little more money from the insurance company, but she stopped fretting about it. She concentrated mostly on her work on the track, and in the field events.

Babe Didrikson began to concentrate all her training and energy toward the national AAU championships. That year the AAU meet and the Olympic tryouts were combined in one meet, which meant that those athletes who won or placed high in the nationals would be put on the Olympic team.

She worked tirelessly to get herself in the finest condition of her young life for the Olympic qualifying meet, to be held in Evanston, Illinois.

She knew, by this time, that she would be the sole representative of the Golden Cyclones at the crucial track and field meet in Dyche Stadium, just outside of Chicago.

To prepare herself for this once-in-a-lifetime opportunity, Babe and Mel McCombs worked out a strenuous training program, which was to get her in the finest condition.

She was up at the crack of dawn each morning running around the track for a mile. She would run the mile as fast as she possibly could. At the end of the first week she increased the distance to two miles, and she pushed and drove herself as she concentrated all her energies in building her strength and endurance for the big meet.

After she completed the morning run she would shower, breakfast, and then take a half-hour nap. Then she was up, dressed once again in her track suit to practice each and every event she would enter.

After her nap she would sprint several 100-yard-dash races against her teammates. Then she would be off to another part of the field to throw the javelin, then the shot put. Then it was another part of the field and the baseball throw; then off to the high jump and the running broad jump. Then it was the discus throw, and last but not least, she would tear through the 80-meter hurdles event against stiff opposition from teammates.

Day after day she pushed herself racing against time and space to whip herself into one superhuman being capable of undergoing the most grueling one-day ordeal any athlete has ever been called upon to perform.

It was a tremendous burden for the young lady, just twenty years old, but there was one man who had supreme confidence in her: Colonel Mel J. McCombs.

He called her into his office one afternoon, late in May.

"Sit down, Babe," he said.

She sat down.

"I want to talk to you about the meet in Evanston."

Babe held her breath.

"Are we canceling out?" she asked, suddenly cold with apprehension.

"No. We're not canceling out," said McCombs.

Babe breathed more easily.

"You've been working and training harder than anyone I've ever known, and you're in marvelous condition.

"I've just been studying the records of the other girls in the meet, the other teams."

He spoke quietly. Babe strained to hear him.

"I think," continued the colonel in his deliberate manner, "that if you give us the kind of performances you've shown in practice the last several weeks, you can do something that no athlete in history has ever done."

Babe was all excited now.

"What's that, Colonel McCombs?" she asked, eagerly.

"I believe you can win the national championship for us," said the colonel, without raising the pitch of his voice one iota. "I think you can win the championship all by yourself.

That also means a place on the U. S. Olympic team. It's a performance that could possibly make you the greatest athlete in the world."

Babe might have cried at this. She didn't.

"Well, I've worked awful hard, Colonel. Full-time during the last three months. I've got my hurdling form almost perfect. I'm throwing the baseball farther every time I throw the ball, and my jumping is good, too. I've yet to miss, cause everyone at home is counting on it," said Babe.

"I think you can, too, Babe. I don't know anyone, male or female, who has worked harder. You've got the qualities to be the best in the world," said Colonel McCombs.

# Chapter 6

FOLLOWING HER triumph in Evanston, Babe Didrikson was named one of the sixteen girls to represent the United States in the 1932 Olympic Games at Los Angeles. Unlike the situation at the Evanston meet, however, where Babe entered and won almost every event, she was limited by the Olympic Committee to three events: the high jump, the hurdles, and the javelin throw. She would have liked to participate in all the events, but she accepted the decision of the Olympic Committee gracefully enough.

The Olympic team traveled in a private railroad car with a huge red-white-and-blue banner that said "U. S. Olympic Team" spread across the length of the train. When the train roared across the plains of Illinois and Kansas toward Denver, hundreds of people turned out to greet the young stars.

Some of Babe's Olympic teammates, however, didn't think her attitude, or her actions, on the train that carried them to Los Angeles, particularly graceful.

Exuberantly, and determined to continue her rigorous training and while the rest of the girls were playing cards, talking, or just enjoying the scenery, Babe Didrikson did calisthenics in the aisles, jogged the length of the train throughout the day. At night before bedtime, more exercises, more sprints up and down the train.

The more kindly disposed girls would call out to her, "Why don't you take it easy?"

There were those who were less kindly disposed.

"She kept running through the train, shrieking and yanking pillows out from under your head if you were sleeping."

"She had no social graces," said another of her teammates. "If one girl said she had paddled from Alaska in a kayak, Babe would horn in and say, 'I did that. I did that in half the time.'"

"She couldn't stand anybody from the press talking to any of the other girls," said a third teammate. "She would always butt in. If that didn't work, she'd take out her harmonica and play it so loud that nobody could talk to anybody."

Incidentally, Babe Didrikson could play that harmonica very well.

One of her teammates recalled the train stop at Albuquerque.

"Babe found a bike and rode it around the station platform yelling, 'Ever hear of Babe Didrikson? You will! You will!'"

Braggadocio or just sheer exuberance, it didn't matter. Babe Didrikson was determined to put on a record-breaking performance at the 1932 Olympics in Los Angeles.

At Olympic City in Los Angeles, she found herself surrounded and applauded by the greatest names in sports and show business. The great Olympic swimmer Eleanor Holm was there, and sprinters Ed Tolan and Frank Wykoff, Ralph Metcalfe and Bill Carr. In Hollywood she met Clark Gable and Will Rogers and Mary Pickford, Doug Fairbanks, Janet Gaynor, and Norma Shearer, Norma Talmadge, Joe E. Brown, and Mickey Rooney.

She met them all and, whether it was her innocence or the

fact that big names never awed her, she was at ease with all of them, and most of the big stars were attracted to the Babe.

She met the leading sportswriters in the nation, too—Grantland Rice, Paul Gallico, Westbrook Pegler, and Braven Dyer—and she was just as relaxed with them as she was with the others. She even went out to play with a foursome on the golf course—Paul Gallico, Damon Runyon, and Wes Pegler—at Grantland Rice's invitation, and she showed them she could drive the ball as far as they could.

"I've never seen a woman who could hit the ball the way you do," said the dean of the sportswriters, Grantland Rice. "You've got the ability to be a great golfer, Babe," he added.

"I will be one day," said the brash young woman, in her manner of the day.

And she would be.

At the moment, even before the opening ceremonies of the 1932 Olympic Games, Babe was already the darling of every reporter in Los Angeles. Sportswriters from every major newspaper in the nation reported her daily doings. She was good copy, and she loved every minute of every day, when the spotlight was on her achievements.

"I am out to beat everybody in sight," she announced at a press conference one afternoon, "and that's just what I'm going to do!"

"I can do anything," she added, "and beat anybody in any one of my track and field events."

The newspapers ate it up, and there were more interviews and more feature stories.

"Folks say that I go about winning these athletic games because I have the co-operation thing that has to do with the eye, mind, and muscle," she expounded. "That is sure a powerful lot of language to use about a girl from Texas, but maybe they're right."

She had a bit of the Will Rogers style in her tongue, too.

"All I know," she went on, to the delight of the sports-writers, "is that I can run and I can jump and I can toss things. And when they fire a gun or tell me to get busy, I just say to myself, 'Well, kid, here's where you've got to win another.'"

It's no wonder that she drew the jealousy from the other girls around her, and it was no wonder that she was the girl every newspaperman, and newspaperwoman, wanted to in-terview.

All this attention and publicity showered on Babe Didrik-son might have been enough to unbalance almost any other athlete. Not Babe. She enjoyed being treated like the most glamorous lady in Hollywood, yet she kept her mind on her objectives. Her objectives were the gold medals they put around the neck of the winners. She wanted those gold medals more than she ever wanted anything else. And she was prepared to win them.

In July 1932 the United States was staggering under the most severe economic depression this nation had ever known. Hunger, poverty, and unemployment were rampant throughout the nation—millions of men were unemployed, and the bread lines established by many cities to feed the poor and unemployed were crowded with husky men, many fairly well dressed, waiting their turn for a free meal. In many cities hundreds of the unemployed men tried to earn a few dollars selling apples on street corners. In Washington, D.C., the nation's capital, some twenty thousand World War I veterans who called themselves the Bonus Expeditionary Force (BEF) had encamped on a huge empty tract of land near the White House to protest their joblessness and to petition Congress to release their bonus money earned for service during World War I. They were driven from their tents and shacks after living in drab poverty and misery for months, by federal troops under command of General Douglas MacArthur.

News headlines reported that Governor Franklin D. Roosevelt of New York had captured the Democratic presidential nomination over former New York Governor Al Smith on the fourth ballot after the exciting Democratic Convention held in Chicago and would challenge the incumbent Republican President, Herbert Hoover.

At first it was feared that the great economic depression gripping the United States and the rest of the world would spell the ruin of the X Olympiad, which extended from July 30 to August 14, 1932, and was scheduled for Los Angeles. The expense of staging the great athletic spectacle would be too big a burden for the California community. Foreign nations would have neither the monies nor the inclination to send husky athletes on tour at such a time. But the superpromotion carried out by the local California Olympic Committee, who spent more than 10 years planning the world's greatest athletic spectacle, forged ahead in the face of the bleak world situation to successfully hoist the five-circled Olympic flag to new heights above the broad field of international athletic competition on a record-breaking scale. The X Olympiad opened on Saturday, July 30, with 105,000 spectators crowding the rebuilt Olympic stadium as Vice President Charles Curtis formally declared the Games open. Ten cannons roared, 150 bands blared, the 5-ringed Olympic flag was hoisted to the peak, hundreds of pigeons were turned loose to circle the sky over the arena, and from the

Olympic torch atop the peristyle of the stadium there sprang up the flame that was to burn night and day until the end of the Olympic gathering.

The next day a young and high-spirited Babe Didrikson marched, with her U.S. teammates, into the Olympic stadium at Los Angeles, to the huge cheering partisan American crowd on hand to witness the opening ceremonies of the 1932 Olympics.

She could feel the thump-thump in her chest, and her mouth hurt from the broad smile that fixed itself on her face. There was only one thing wrong. She grew more and more uncomfortable in her uniform. The girls on the American team had to wear special dresses, issued by the Olympic Committee. Babe would have preferred her track attire. Worse, she had to wear the white stockings they gave her, and white shoes. She had never worn stockings in her life. She wore anklets and socks. As for the shoes, they had high heels, and Babe always wore flats. The shoes were killing her.

For an hour, she had to stand in the hot August sun, listening to all the routine speeches with which all the Olympic Games routinely begin.

She couldn't take those shoes for another minute. Surreptitiously, she kicked one foot out of one shoe, then the other foot out of the other shoe.

Some of the girls noticed what she did, and pretty soon practically every girl in that American contingent had her feet free from the torturing footwear.

If the Olympic Committee didn't like it, they never complained. And no one could blame them for saying nothing about it. It would take brave men indeed to take on that whole crew of young American women athletes.

Babe gave the Committee—and some of the officials, too—other headaches during the 1932 Olympics.

George Vreeland was the coach for the women's track and field squad. Like any other coach, he tried to mold the form and style of his athletes, give them pointers, try to correct a flaw. Babe Didrikson would have none of it.

Colonel McCombs had made a point of telling Babe to stick to her natural style, and she had done well enough with that bit of advice. She meant to keep it.

"Sorry," she said to Coach Vreeland, "this is the way I've always run the hurdles, thrown the shot. I'm not going to change now."

Vreeland argued. He even pleaded. It did no good.

"There is no one way to do anything in athletics," said Babe Didrikson, much later on. "Every athlete has to find a style, method that works best for him or her."

"O.K.," said Vreeland. "Do it your way."

She did, and she made all of America proud with what she did in those 1932 Olympic Games in Los Angeles.

Her first test came in the javelin throw, and her first throw brought a gasp from the huge crowd in the stadium, followed, an instant later, by a huge roar of approval.

Her first try wasn't a classic throw. It resembled in no way what might be called good form. Her throw did not rise more than twelve feet above the ground, but it flew, like an arrow shot out of a bow, for 143 feet, 4 inches, a new world record. No other competitor in the event came near it. The Babe had won her first Olympic gold medal.

The reporters, who had never seen the javelin thrown the way Babe Didrikson threw it, cluttered around her. They wanted to know all she could tell them about this new technique she had introduced.

"No new technique," said the amused young athlete. "My hand slipped when I picked up the pole," she explained, the big grin on her face. "It slid along six inches, then I got a good grip on it again."

"And then what?" asked the eager newsmen.

"And then I threw it," said Babe.

"Is that it?" pressed the sportswriters.

"That's it," said Babe. "I threw it and it went. It went pretty good, didn't it?" she added, and left the reporters dazed at the sheer power of her effort.

Years later Babe revealed that she was so eager to throw the javelin she had not warmed up properly. "Nobody knew it, but I tore a cartilage in my right shoulder on the first throw," she said, "and it hurt for the rest of the year."

On the fifth day of the Olympics, Babe had to face some stiff competition in the 8o-meter hurdles. Her competitor was another fine young American athlete, Evelyne Hall. Both Evelyne and Babe won their separate heats in world-record time. They raced side by side in the finals.

It was Evelyne Hall by a stride, going over the first two hurdles. Then Babe, to the rising roar of the crowds, began to close the gap. Evelyne was the more graceful hurdler. Babe was more powerful.

As they approached the last two hurdles, the two girls were neck and neck, head and head. There wasn't half an inch between them as they raced for the tape. They seemed to hit the tape together. No one could be sure of the winner.

The judges went into a huddle. Apparently they weren't sure of the winner either.

For some reason she could never explain, Evelyne Hall held up two fingers, as if she were conceding the race to Babe, accepting the fact that she had come in second.

Whatever the case, that is the way the judges decided: Babe Didrikson first, Hall second. Babe had won her second gold Olympic medal.

No woman, from any country, had ever won three gold medals at the Olympics.

The reporters were quick to relay this bit of information to young Didrikson.

"Watch me," said Babe. "Tomorrow it's the high jump, and tomorrow I'll be the first woman to make it three."

She was confident and brash enough, and the sports pages were rich with the accomplishments of Babe Didrikson and the prophecy that she would prove to be the first woman Olympian to bring home the prized three gold medallions. The crowd concentrated on the event and, almost unanimously, pulled for the girl from Texas to make it.

There were some, however, who hoped and even prayed that she would lose. Mostly they were her rivals who were annoyed, irritated, and angered by the publicity the Babe was getting as well as by her success.

Again, Babe Didrikson's rival for the gold medal in the high jump was a young American athlete, Jean Shiley. It was the same Jean Shiley who had tied Babe in the high jump at the qualifying meet in Evanston.

By the time the high-jump bar had been raised to 5 feet, 5 inches, everyone but Babe and Jean dropped out of the competition.

Babe cleared the 5 feet, 5 inches.

So did Jean Shiley.

This was two inches higher than the record they had both beaten at Evanston. They had each established a new world record.

The bar was raised. It was raised again.

The bar now stood at 5 feet, 5¾ inches.

Jean Shiley gave it everything she had, but missed.

It was Babe's turn.

Her approach was beautiful. She leaped high into the air . . .

A wild shout roared through the stadium as her body went over the bar by at least four inches; then the shout, as suddenly as it had come, turned to a groan.

"It was the most astonishing jump a woman had ever made," wrote Grantland Rice.

As the Babe came down on the other side of the bar, her left foot struck one of the standards of the high-jump apparatus just a glancing blow; and the crossbar just toppled down.

There was no second try at 5 feet, 5¾ inches.

The bar was dropped back to 5 feet, 5 inches.

This jump was to decide the gold medal and the championship.

Jean Shiley cleared the crossbar cleanly.

So did Babe.

It looked like a tie again.

But no!

Babe Didrikson had used a style that most high jumpers, amateur and professional, use to this day, the western roll; at least it looked like a modification of the western roll. The judges ruled that her head had cleared the crossbar first, and her body followed.

"Illegal," they said. "We'll have to rule out Babe's jump."

"Illegal," said the judges. "Jean Shiley is the new champion."

Their decision was final.

Babe didn't get that third gold medal she wanted so much. The gold medal went to an almost hysterically happy Jean Shiley. Babe got the silver medal.

Babe was disappointed, of course. She let everybody know about it in a string of well-chosen words in which she gave her excoriating views on all track officials and judges. But she accepted the silver medal for second place in the Olympic high jump with considerable grace.

There was one bit of consolation for the young woman from Dallas. She was officially recognized as the co-owner of a new world high-jump record.

Two gold medals, one silver medal—Babe Didrikson was unquestionably the greatest woman athlete at those 1932 Olympics. For a good many, among them the top sports-writers in the business, she was the greatest athlete of them all at the Olympics, male or female.

"She is an incredible human being," wrote the dean of sports columnists, Grantland Rice. "She is beyond all belief until you see her perform. Then you finally understand that you are looking at the most flawless section of muscle harmony, of complete mental and physical co-ordination the world of sport has ever known. There is only one Babe Didrikson, and there has never been another in her class— even close to her class."

With reports like that ringing in her ears and pumping her blood till it raced, Babe Didrikson returned home to Dallas, where the entire city was prepared to give her as great a welcome as any American city ever gave to a home-coming, conquering hero.

The mayor was at the Love Field airport to greet her. So were all the other official dignitaries of the city. Homer R. Mitchell, president of Employers Casualty Insurance Company, was there, of course. So was Colonel Mel McCombs, who embraced Babe as she stepped off the plane. Mamma and Papa Didrikson and all the family were there, too, after traveling all night from Beaumont in their rundown jalopy of a car.

There were speeches at Love Field, and music.

"It's good to be home," yelled the Olympic heroine, and the huge crowd at Love Field yelled back its approval.

They brought up the gleaming red limousine of the Dallas fire chief. The car flowed over with roses. With the top down, they drove her through the streets of Dallas, slowly, so all the men, women, and children lining the sidewalks two and three deep could get a good look at their Olympic champion.

And the crowd threw confetti and streamers at her, the way they always do at the parade for a national hero. They shredded paper, newspaper, any kind of paper, and tossed that out into the street and over the motorcade in their enthusiasm, as an excited and elated Babe Didrikson waved her arms and hands in saluting her shouting and applauding admirers.

There were more flowers in the Adolphus Hotel, where the city had provided a suite of rooms for the homecoming heroine. There were more flowers on all the tables at the big dinner they threw for her.

It was a day Babe Didrikson would never forget. It was a day all Dallas would not forget.

It was also the day that would prove the beginning of the end of Babe's stay in that hustling, bustling Texas city. Greater things were on the horizon for Babe Didrikson. And that horizon was not too far away.

At the end of 1932 the Associated Press poll of sportswriters and broadcasters chose Babe as the Woman Athlete of the Year. It was just one of the honors she was to win for herself year after year after year.

# Chapter 7

BABE DIDRIKSON's salary at Employers Casualty Insurance Company had been increased to $90 a month. But now that $90-a-month clerk had become a national celebrity. For fully two years after her great performance at the 1932 Olympics, there was an endless stream of stories and photographs about her in the sport pages of the daily newspapers, in the whole range of sports magazines that cluttered the newsstands. The merest piece of gossip was enough for a story. Her least gesture was enough for a full-length feature in a magazine. Even the biggest national magazines, *The Saturday Evening Post* and *Collier's,* gave pages of space to satisfy the avid appetites of their readers for news, biographical notes, and more news about America's great athletic queen.

Often as not, the sportswriters and the feature writers, for lack of something concrete to write about, would invent stories.

"Babe Didrikson is reported to be training to become a marathon swimmer. She intends to swim the English Channel and the Hellespont."

"Corrida *aficionados* have been promised by Mexican officials that Babe Didrikson will travel south of the border to make her debut as a bullfighter in a Mexican ring."

"A prominent designer of clothes in England asserts that Babe Didrikson will appear in London as a high-fashion model."

"Hollywood is knocking at Babe Didrikson's door. Every studio in Hollywood wants to sign her up to a long-term and lucrative contract."

"Babe Didrikson has been offered $65,000 a year to play professional basketball."

There may have been some bit of truth in these news items but, at best, they were exaggerations.

She did get a letter from the Illinois Women's Athletic Club, offering her a job paying $300 a month, if she quit Employers Casualty Insurance Company and joined the Illinois club. Nothing of this appeared in the press.

Nor did the press print the story of how Babe got the Dallas insurance company to match that bid.

The Babe simply took that letter and showed it to the president of the Texas outfit, which was still paying her the grand sum of $90 a month.

Homer R. Mitchell, president of the Dallas company, read the letter and, without a change of expression, offered to match the Illinois bid.

"Why, Babe," he said, "I think we can give you $300 a month if you stay here."

Babe stayed, but not for long.

There was another story that didn't hit the press—so one could notice it, anyway.

Amelia Earhart, the legendary American aviatrix, was planning one of her long-distance flights. She asked Babe to join her. Amelia Earhart was as publicity-conscious as any figure in the public eye. She knew that if she could get Babe to travel with her on her scheduled flight, she'd get front-page national publicity in every paper and magazine in the country. Besides—and this was no small matter—Amelia Earhart really liked and respected the young athlete.

But flying wasn't for Babe Didrikson, not just yet. Amelia Earhart actually pleaded with the younger woman to accompany her on her flight, but Babe couldn't be persuaded. The only flying Babe cared for at that moment was the flight she took over the high-jump crossbars, or the broad jump, or the flight of the baseball, the javelin, the discus, as she hurled them through the air.

It was inevitable that Babe's fall from the headlines started when the AAU questioned her amateur status in November 1932.

"Amateur Athletic Union Questions Babe Didrikson Amateur Standing," read the headlines on the sports pages.

The object of the AAU investigation was the Dodge red coupe she acquired after returning from the Olympics. The car cost $835. Babe had made no down payment on the coupe and had arranged to pay for it in installments of $69 a month. She was earning just $90 a month at the time, and the AAU wanted to know how she could live on the $11 she had left after paying that $69 installment. They also wanted to know why the automobile dealer had waived the down payment on the car.

That was the beginning of a complicated story. It got worse.

Some bright young man working for the advertising agency handling the Dodge account had a bright idea; at least it was a bright idea as far as the Dodge people were concerned. It almost wrecked a great career, if only for a little while.

The young ad man's idea was to have a picture of the

Dodge red coupe, a duplicate of Babe's car, accompanied by a picture of Babe, and her endorsement.

This was the ad everyone in America saw. The AAU saw it, too, and it acted on it at once. They ruled that Babe Didrikson had violated her amateur standing, and they suspended her from participating in any AAU competition, indefinitely.

Babe Didrikson protested vigorously.

"I never gave them permission to print my picture," she declared. "I never gave them permission to print what I said."

What she had said, according to the ad, was, "Speed—unyielding strength—enduring stamina—that's the stuff that makes real champions, whether they're in the athletic arena or in the world of automobiles."

Anyone who knew Babe knew that those printed words could never have come out of the Babe's mouth.

Paul Gallico, protesting the AAU suspension of Babe Didrikson, wrote in his columns, "If Babe said what the salesman said she said, I'll eat one of her javelins with mustard."

He didn't have to.

The Dodge people wired the AAU.

They admitted, or at least declared, that Babe's statements concerning the Dodge advertisement were completely true. They said that their car salesman had simply remembered Babe's enthusiasm for the car and that he had noted down, word for word, what she had said about it.

"Babe Didrikson," the wire to the AAU continued, "never gave us permission to print those words. She never gave us permission to print her picture."

The AAU may have accepted that wire as convincing evidence of the truth, the whole truth, about the automobile transaction. More likely they reacted to the national protests against the suspension of the young heroine of the Olympics. In either case, it was only a matter of weeks before they lifted the "indefinite" suspension and restored Babe Didrikson to full amateur status.

Babe, of course, along with the rest of America's sports lovers, was delighted. Ironically, however, it was only a few days after her reinstatement that Babe deserted the amateur ranks.

She handed in her resignation at the offices of the Employers Casualty Insurance Company and went to work for the Chrysler Corporation, not as an athlete, but as an adjunct to their sales force.

Actually, her first and only job with the automobile company was to draw people to the Dodge display at the Auto Show in Detroit.

She talked to people. She signed autographs. She even played her harmonica when the crowd around her stand thinned out, to build it up again. It is said that she did a memorable imitation of a locomotive leaving a railroad station.

People at the Auto Show knew who she was and were delighted to talk with her and come away with the great athlete's autograph. But the Dodge booth was a long way from track and field. These couldn't have been the happiest days in the young life of Babe Didrikson. It must have given her a bad turn to read in newspaper stories of "great athletes of the past" that she was already considered a "has-been."

However, it would seem that the Babe was not terribly concerned about the turn of events. In Detroit, with her sister Esther Nancy as chaperone, she met the president of the Chrysler Corporation, K. T. Keller, along with the other officers of the organization. They had set her up in a suite of rooms in the elegant Book Cadillac Hotel. They had treated her like a heroine, flowers, dinners, theater, and all the rest that goes with it. They had even appointed a man out of the Ruthrauff and Ryan advertising agency, a George P. Emerson, to act as her personal agent. Emerson's responsibility, at no fee at all to Babe, was to get her personal booking, theatrical books, sports appearances, and the like.

To a still naïve Babe Didrikson, though she truly missed all those columns about her feats in the sports pages, the world was a picture of great possibilities. The future, as Babe saw it at that moment, was one bright path of joy and glory.

It was not as bright as all that, as she was soon to discover. But, in addition to all her other good attributes, skill, determination, and the will to win, Babe was endowed with the ability to endure.

She would endure much before she would rise again to the pinnacle she achieved at the 1932 Olympics; and then she would find herself in even rarer atmospheres of success.

# Chapter 8

THE FIRST booking her agent got for Babe was on the RKO vaudeville circuit, an eighteen-minute act at the RKO Palace Theater in Chicago.

She was considered a star attraction and got top billing, even though the celebrated movie star Fifi D'Orsay was appearing in the same show. Babe even got the star dressing room.

At first, seeing the big crowd lined around the block, waiting to get into the theater, Babe got the jitters.

"My Lord," she said to herself, "I can't go through with this!"

But, always the good trouper, she did.

She had a fellow by the name of George Libbey as part of her act. He was a vaudevillian. He knew how to set the stage for the star.

He played the piano and did an imitation of Eddie Cantor to warm up the audience; then Babe Didrikson made her appearance to a tumultuous welcome.

She came down the center aisle, out of the audience, in high-heeled shoes, a green swagger coat, and a panama hat. She was supposed to be someone just back from a vacation in Florida.

Babe and her partner, George Libbey, swapped a couple

of routine vaudeville gags, then Babe went into her song, "I'm Fit as a Fiddle and Ready for Love," to which she added a couple of "boop-boop-a-dee-dees" in the manner, at the time, of the great crooner Bing Crosby.

Next in the act came the treadmill. She took off her high-heeled shoes and put on a pair of rubber-soled track shoes. She threw off her green swagger coat and, to the applause and whistles of the audience, revealed the red-white-and-blue jacket she was wearing, and the silk satin shorts. For the audience she was the epitome of the American Olympic girl, and they applauded wildly.

She jogged the treadmill, set up against a black velvet backdrop, faster and faster, evidently to show her Olympic style; and she would end this part of her act by breaking the tape—the winner again.

The audience loved it.

She jumped the hurdles set on the stage, as another part of her act. She played her harmonica for a change of pace. Then, for a finale, she drove plastic golf balls into the audience.

End of the act, and an audience ovation.

Clark Rodenbach, reviewing the act for the Chicago *Tribune*, was as enthusiastic about the performance as anyone else in the theater.

"Friday afternoon was the Babe's first time behind footlights," he wrote, "and the girl from the Lone Star State took the hurdle as gallantly as she ever did on the track."

RKO scheduled shows for Babe in Brooklyn and Manhattan. They were so pleased with her reception at the RKO Palace Theater in Chicago that they were ready to send her on the entire RKO circuit, throughout the country.

But Babe was having second thoughts. She enjoyed stepping out onto the stage, entertaining the big crowds at the theater, and she certainly enjoyed the plaudits of both the audience and the reviewers. It was the routine of being a vaudevillian that bothered her.

"I'm spending all my time in the theater or in a hotel room," she complained to her sister Esther Nancy. "This isn't my kind of life."

"You're making a lot of money in the theater," said Nancy. Babe was drawing $2,500 a week for her act.

"I don't want the money if I have to make it this way," said Babe, obviously unhappy.

"That's something you'll have to decide yourself," said Nancy.

"I think I ought to quit," said Babe. "My life is outdoors— track, golf, anything but this indoor business."

Nancy wouldn't argue with that.

Nor would Babe's agent, George Emerson.

RKO canceled the Brooklyn and Manhattan appearances. They understood Babe's point of view and sympathized with it. They released her from her contract with them.

She went on to New York anyway. She didn't know what she was going to do there, but New York was the big town, and things do happen there.

She called a press conference.

The press, still eager for stories on Babe, of which there hadn't been too many of late, attended in force.

She announced that she and Babe Ruth might put on a sparring match at McGovern's gym the following afternoon.

How much truth there was in this announcement, nobody knows. The two Babes had met at one time, some time ago. Babe Didrikson would meet all the great sports stars in her time. She had met Jack Dempsey, when he came to the theater in Chicago to see her act, and they were to remain friends for the rest of her life. But Babe Ruth probably never heard of the sparring match Babe Didrikson had evidently dreamed up.

The idea of the match made some good publicity for both Babes, but on the afternoon they were supposed to meet in McGovern's gym, neither one of them appeared.

She did play an exhibition billiard game with Ruth McGinnis, a professional billiard player, in New York. Babe also played her first professional game of basketball, for a fee of $400.

The Babe played for the Brooklyn Yankees. Their opponents were the Long Island Ducklings. The game was played in a Brooklyn dance hall, before a crowd of some two thousand fans.

The Ducklings were a rough-and-tough organization.

"I never got pushed around and fouled so much in any basketball game," said Babe.

The Long Island girls were evidently set to show Babe Didrikson the difference between amateur and professional ball. Their playing was what one might call a bit "dirty."

Toward the end of the first half, Babe's pants were split partway up the side. It was that rough.

"Everybody thought that I'd change my pants during halftime," said Babe, "but I wasn't going to change. I was all fired up to get back on the floor, to show these girls they couldn't stop me no matter how rough they played the game."

This was the old Babe Didrikson come to life.

"When we came out for the second half and the people saw me still wearing those torn pants, they cheered and yelled," she said.

"Come on, Babe! Show 'em, Babe!"

The Babe broke loose.

"At one point," she related, "I took the ball at center court and dribbled all the way through the clawing Ducklings to lay the ball in for a score. I jumped so high and hard going in for the basket that my arm hit the backboard, and I wound up in somebody's lap about six rows back."

The Brooklyn Yankees won that game, beating the Long Island Ducklings, 19–16. Scores ran very low in the basketball games of those days. Of those 19 Brooklyn Yankees' points, Babe Didrikson had scored 9. She had well earned her $400 fee.

There would be more professional basketball for the Babe.

Ray Doan, a promoter out of Muscatine, Iowa, thought up the idea of a Babe Didrikson All-Americans basketball squad. The difficulty was in how to put the team together.

They got one girl by the name of Jane Mitchell and, for a while, one other girl to join them; but that made only three, and a basketball team needs a nucleus of five, plus reserve players.

Doan and Babe settled that problem by recruiting men to fill out the roster of Babe Didrikson's All-Americans, and they toured the country, playing against local men's teams around the country.

According to Babe, "We weren't world-beaters, but we had a pretty fair bunch of basketball players. Generally we made out all right, playing whatever opposition we ran into."

Whatever the case, wherever Babe Didrikson's All-Americans appeared, and especially in the Midwest, they drew large and enthusiastic crowds. Babe was still the big attraction, and she pocketed $2,000 a month for it. That was a fantastic amount of money for those days, when women were being paid as little as $2.50 per week for a full week's work. Each week as quickly as she could, Babe would go to the local bank and cash the check, keep a few dollars for her weekly expenses, and mail the balance to her folks in Beaumont. She was endlessly generous with her family and constantly sent home expensive gifts. She bought her father a new Dodge in 1933. She sent home birthday gifts for each member of the family. Once she arranged a birthday party for Mamma and arranged to deliver a new stove and refrigerator. When her dad became ill in 1933, Babe took care of all the bills. She bought dresses for Lillian and would send home endless baskets of fruit and other foods. "I was the best-dressed girl in Beaumont when Babe was alive," says Lillian.

In the spring of 1934, Babe, still searching for a more permanent pursuit for herself, stopped off at Brandenton, Florida, where the St. Louis Cardinals were doing their spring training that year. The Cardinals were scheduled to play the Philadelphia Athletics in an exhibition game, and Babe was sitting in the stands with those two great pitchers, Dizzy and Daffy Dean, of the St. Louis Cardinals, and with Jimmy Foxx of the Athletics.

Dizzy was ribbing Jimmy Foxx.

"We'll pitch Babe against you," he drawled in his southern manner, "and I'll betcha me and Paul and Babe can beat you guys."

"You're on," said Jimmy Foxx, as eager as anybody for an easy bet.

So, for a lark, for the publicity, for $200, Babe Didrikson took the mound to pitch against the Philadelphia Athletics for Frankie Frisch's St. Louis Cardinals.

Babe had good control. She didn't walk anybody.

The first three A's who came to the plate reached base. They didn't hit anything hard, but they were hitting cleanly, and they loaded the bases with three straight singles.

Even an old pro might have been perturbed by the situation: bases loaded and nobody out. But the Babe calmly strode up to the pitching rubber, took the full windup, and came in fast with the pitch.

The batter took a full cut and hit the ball sharply, a hot line drive that should have scored at least two of the Athletics on base. It didn't.

Before Babe Didrikson could turn around to look where the ball had gone, second baseman Dick Williams snared the ball in his glove, tagged the runner leading off second, then tripped and tagged the other base runner for a triple play. The next day she agreed to pitch for the Cardinals against the Philadelphia Athletics.

Babe Didrikson should have been awed, as the first three batters all hit safely. The next batter smashed into a double play.

There were two outs and she calmly toed the rubber again, took her signal from her catcher, and pitched the ball hard to Jimmy Foxx.

Foxx, one of the greatest sluggers of all time, got hold of it and sent it deep, deep, deep.

Paul (Daffy) Dean, who was playing the outfield that afternoon, went back deep, deep, deep into the orange grove that fenced in the playing field; and he came out of that orange grove with the ball in his glove. He had caught it, along with half a dozen oranges in his mitt.

That was the end of the inning.

"And that was enough pitching for me that day," said Babe Didrikson.

She pitched once more for the St. Louis Cardinals that spring, in an exhibition game against the Boston Red Sox. She did a pretty good job of it, too. Bucky Harris, the Red Sox manager, was impressed, as were the rest of Boston's ball team.

"She can handle that ball as good as some of our pitchers," said Bucky Harris appreciatively.

She could, and she did, that summer, but not in the big leagues.

Ray Doan, a baseball promoter, signed Babe for a nation-wide tour with the House of David baseball team. It may have been a novelty for a woman to appear with all those ball players sporting full-grown beards, and the appearance of Babe Didrikson did much to enhance the drawing power of this colorful team. Babe was not the only star on the team. Grover Cleveland Alexander, a former major-league pitcher, was also a star attraction. Babe and Alex would each pitch a few innings. Babe was a fair pitcher, and an outstanding hitter. One day in a game at Chicago's Logan Field, Babe drove out a home run to win a 1–0 game.

It was a grueling pace for Babe that summer. She played in two hundred games and was always on the move. The schedule for the House of David carried her from Fort Lauderdale in Florida to the heart of Iowa. She was glad when the baseball season came to an end, for she was drained, physically and emotionally.

It was time to go home, to rest, and to do some thinking and planning for her future.

She knew that the reputation she had built up for herself at the Olympics was fading, fading fast, if it was not entirely gone. She had to think about why so much of the glamour that had been hers, was all but gone. She had to re-evaluate all future activities. She must use a positive approach in everything in order to regain her fast fading glamour and reputation. She could not now or ever again lend her good name in a circus-type promotion.

There was the need to evaluate her appearances at the theater, her professional basketball game, her baseball experience with the House of David. She began to seriously direct her real attitude toward the game of golf, which she had only played at but never really seriously.

More than all else, she realized that she would have to make a decision that would fix the course of the rest of her life. She had to choose a profession.

She knew that the profession had to be a sport. Sports were her life. But which one?

It often happens that an accidental meeting, an incidental experience, will move a person into a particular career, a particular life-style.

And this is what happened with Babe Didrikson, except that it was a man she idolized in addition, which led Babe to decide the path she would walk the rest of her life.

It was a perfect choice, and the path she chose was destined to bring her the kind of rewards that perhaps even the Babe had not dreamed of.

# Chapter 9

BABE HAD made a considerable amount of money, playing the Palace Theater in Chicago, appearing in exhibition matches, playing for the Brooklyn Yankees, barnstorming with Babe Didrikson's All-Americans and the House of David baseball team. She wasn't exactly a big spender, except for the automobiles she loved so much, but she took good care of her family. She showered them all with gifts.

She bought suits for Papa Didrikson and all the khaki shirts and pants he wanted. She bought her mamma a whole wardrobe of dresses. She also bought her a new stove and refrigerator. She even had the house on Doucette fixed and enlarged.

Her sister Lillie got her wedding gown from Babe, and shoes and dresses, and even furs. Babe didn't neglect anyone in the family when she went shopping for gifts for them, which was often enough.

Still, Ruth Scurlock, who was as friendly with Babe as was her sportswriting husband, remarked that not all the members of Babe's family were as grateful as they might have been for Babe's generosity.

"They got bitter," she said, "when she did not give them more, more, more. They had their hands out all the time."

Evidently, Babe did not think of her giving as a generosity. She seemed to assume the business of giving as something like a duty.

In any case, in addition to worrying about what steps she needed to take to regain her good name in the sports world, she fretted about the need to make a lot of money.

"There had to be money," she said, "not only for me, but for the family."

She thought of tennis. Tennis wasn't the popular spectator sport it is today. The leading professionals had to scratch for a living. Still, with some kind of foresight, the Babe saw tennis as a good potential money-maker. She tried her hand at it.

She practiced the forehand stroke and was pretty good at it. She practiced the backhand. It was a good backhand. Babe began to grow enthusiastic about the possibilities of the game. She could already see, in her mind, the stands jammed with people come to see her play.

She began to work on her serve, and here the whole dream of a great tennis career collapsed.

It wasn't that she couldn't hit the ball hard enough, or send it into the right side of the court. It was her arm. She couldn't raise it properly. She had torn the cartilage in her right shoulder hurling the javelin at the Olympic Games. She thought nothing of it, expecting it to heal with time. But it hadn't healed—at least it hadn't yet healed quite right.

Babe didn't give up, not right away. She tried, and the pain was sharp. She tried again, and the pain was sharper. She would have tried again, but it was just impossible for her to lift that right arm. Babe had to give up tennis, but it was perhaps for the best, as time would prove.

Bobby Jones, that all-time great golfer, who had made a

grand slam of the British and American Amateur and Open golf tournaments in 1930, was scheduled to play an exhibition game at the Houston Country Club.

Babe, and a lot of other folks from around the country, would travel miles to see the great Bobby in action. And Babe was eager to see him play for two reasons.

First, forced to give up the idea of becoming a tennis pro, Babe began to think more and more of the possibilities the golf game offered her.

Second, in Babe's own words, "Bobby Jones was a great idol of mine."

The weather wasn't good. The skies were dark with clouds, and there was an imminent threat of rain. But Babe was in that crowd that watched Bobby tee off.

From the start, Babe loved what she saw.

"He just stepped up there on the tee," she said, "and slugged the ball."

Slugging was Babe's style. Bobby Jones played the game the way she liked it.

There were just a couple of holes that Jones played that afternoon before the rain came down in buckets on Houston. But those two or three holes were enough to get Babe's adrenalin going again. Her mind was made up: She was going to play golf. She was going to make a career of it. And she was going to be the best in the game.

But first she had to get that money she needed for herself and her family.

She settled that problem quickly.

Employers Casualty Insurance Company of Dallas was glad to have the Babe back with them. They hired her on the spot for the same $300 a month she had been getting from them. They did more. They got her a membership in the Dallas Country Club. And more. They paid for the lessons George Aulbach, the club's pro, gave her.

She was at the club morning, noon, and night. She practiced hitting the ball until her hands were swollen and tender to the touch. Then one day, she loaded her sister and mother into her little red Dodge and drove to Los Angeles. Stan Kertes, a young professional golfer who taught Al Jolson, Harold Lloyd, and Burns and Allen, took Babe in hand and had her hit golf balls five, six, even eight hours a day. She would hit . . . hit . . . hit until her hands were sore and bleeding. Then she would tape them up and continue to practice. Several months went by until she felt that she was ready for her first tournament.

By November of 1934 she felt she was ready to take on the leading professionals in the Southwest. She entered the Fort Worth Women's Invitational tournament.

Babe's name may have faded a bit from the sports pages, but she was still a celebrity whenever a reporter talked with her.

"How are you doing, Babe?"

"What are you doing, Babe?"

"I'm going to play professional golf."

"How do you think you'll make out?" they asked her.

"I haven't been playing too long," she replied, and she seemed to be counting the holes. "Let's say I think I could shoot a 77. That ought to win for me."

It all seems pretty much like a prelude to Muhammad Ali, in retrospect. Ali, the Greatest, would predict the round in which he would take a fight by a knockout. Babe was predicting the score she would turn in for her first effort in a golf tournament.

Curiously, Muhammad Ali's predictions, particularly in

his earlier years and for the most part, proved to be accurate.

Strangely enough, so did Babe Didrikson's prediction at the Fort Worth Women's Invitational. She went out on that qualifying round, the first day of her first big tournament, and after playing the eighteen holes, her tally sheet read exactly 77 strokes.

This was too good a story to waste. Not only had Babe come in with the exact score she had predicted, but she had also won the qualifying medal of the tournament, 5 strokes ahead of the nearest woman in the field.

"Wonder Girl Makes Her Debut in Tournament Golf," read the headlines on the sports pages.

"Babe Turns in a 77!"

"It was like 1932 all over again," said Babe Didrikson, elated.

Here was all the glamour that had once been hers back again.

"How do you get so much distance in your drive?" one of the women competing in the tourney asked her.

"You've got to loosen your girdle to hit them that far," responded the Babe.

She was—for the moment, anyway—her brash young self again.

Babe didn't do so well in the rest of the tournament. As a matter of fact, she was eliminated in one of the early rounds. But she wasn't discouraged. On the contrary, she recognized that she was only at the beginning of her game, and she was more determined than ever to become the greatest woman golfer in America.

# Chapter 10

THE TEXAS STATE WOMEN'S GOLF CHAMPIONSHIP was scheduled to take place at the River Oaks Country Club in Houston in the spring of 1935. Babe Didrikson began to prepare herself for that tournament right after the first of the year, in January, 3½ months before the meet.

"It was terribly important for me to win that tournament," she said.

Babe didn't say, but she felt she must win that tournament if she were going to continue her career as a pro golfer.

"I never prepared myself for anything the way I did for that Texas golf championship," she said. "I settled into as tough a siege as I've ever gone through for any sports event in my life. Tougher."

The Babe knew that there was much she had to learn about the game. She also knew that practice would be her best teacher.

Every morning she was up at dawn, practicing with every club, every shot in the book from about five-thirty till eight-thirty, when it was time for her to get to work at Employers Casualty.

At lunchtime, she ate her sandwich quickly, then moved into her boss's office to practice some more.

"The boss had the only office with a carpet," Babe explained.

He was kind enough, or enthusiastic enough about Babe's golf, to let her use it.

"I practiced putting on the carpet," said Babe.

She also chipped balls into her boss's leather chair, which, considerately, they had moved away from the window and into a corner of the office.

The mirror in her boss's closet gave Babe the opportunity to practice her grip and check on it.

Back to work after lunch. Babe was in the office till three-thirty, when she was free to go to the Dallas Country Club. There she would take an hour of instruction from the club pro, George Aulbach, after which she just continued to practice and hit, hit, hit golf balls until she could scarcely hold the clubs.

"My hands were bloody and sore," said Babe. "I'd tape up the sores, and the blood would ooze out of the tape."

At night Babe would retire to her bed, but not from golf. She had the tournament golf rule book in her hands and she would read through those rules till her eyes just shut on her.

It was a tough routine that the Babe set for herself, but so was the goal that occupied her, body, mind, and soul, those days, weeks, and months before the Texas State Women's Golf championship.

Babe arrived in Houston about the fifteenth of April. The tournament was scheduled to start on the twenty-second, but Babe wanted to get to know the course at the River Oaks Country Club as well as she could before she teed off in the match.

Jack Burke, the pro at the club, was helpful.

"How was it?" he would ask, as Babe finished a practice eighteen holes.

"Not bad," Babe would say, "but I don't like the way I was using my No. 3 iron."

"Let's work on it," Jack Burke would suggest.

And he was good enough to help Babe work out her flaws with the No. 3 iron, with any of the irons, with her wood, with her putter.

"He's one of the many fine men I've been indebted to over the years," said Babe, "for showing me how to improve my golf."

Babe was tense as the qualifying round for the Texas championship got under way, but her game was good. She shot an 84. Peggy Chandler, a big star, shot a 79 to lead the field. Peggy Chandler was a great golfer. She was the favorite to take the championship. She had finished one-two in the previous three Texas State championships at Houston.

Thirty-two women qualified for the tournament. Thirty-two women went into match play.

Mrs. James Hutchinson of Houston was Babe Didrikson's first opponent. The Babe beat her, six holes up with five to play.

The sports pages once again commented very favorably on Babe's long tee shots, but they questioned whether Babe was a match for Mrs. Walter Woodul of Houston, her second opponent in the tournament.

There was a large gallery to watch Babe tee off in her first match, and to follow her around the course. There was an even larger gallery of golf fans to watch her tee off against Mrs. Woodul.

It may have been the gallery that inspired Babe to a magnificent performance that afternoon. The gallery seemed to be always behind the Babe, cheering her on. Or it may be that all this obvious support for Babe was disturbing to Mrs. Woodul.

In either case, Mrs. Woodul proved no match for Babe Didrikson. Babe just went out and beat Mrs. Woodul eight up with six holes to play.

Mrs. F. C. Rochon, of Wichita Falls in North Texas, was a tougher opponent in the quarterfinals of the tournament. But Babe took that match, too.

For the semifinals, Babe was matched up against Mrs. R. E. Winger of Fort Worth, and their match proved to be perhaps the most dramatic of the entire tournament.

The day was dark with clouds. There was an intermittent rain during the first nine holes of play. And it was windy.

Babe was two up at the end of the first nine holes, when the rains came down in earnest and messed up the whole course. The two women decided to wait for the weather to ease up.

They waited a long time, hours. The course was still pretty much a mess when they teed off again, at the tenth hole.

At the tenth hole, Mrs. Winger cut Babe's lead to one up. Mrs. Winger won the fifteenth hole and the match was tied.

The match was still tied as Babe and Mrs. Winger went for the eighteenth and last hole of the course. The gallery around them, despite the miserable weather, was huge.

Babe teed off. It was a long drive, but it went off the fairway and into the trees on the right. The gallery groaned.

Mrs. Winger teed off. Her drive was not as long as Babe's, but it was right down the middle—a fine shot.

Babe's second shot got her onto the fairway. Mrs. Winger's second shot was in the rough.

Each woman was on the green with her third shot. Babe was about twenty feet from the cup. Mrs. Winger was about twenty-two, twenty-three feet from the hole.

The gallery was quiet, tense.

Mrs. Winger measured the distance, then putted a beautiful shot to the very edge of the cup.

The gallery had a problem keeping quiet.

It was Babe's turn. She took her putter, swung the club back and forth, quickly tapped the ball sharply toward the hole.

It was an uphill putt, and the ground was just soppy with the rain that had fallen.

The ball moved up the hill smartly. It kept going and going and, as the gallery of fans let out a mighty yell, the ball fell into the cup.

Babe Didrikson had won the semifinals by one tremendous putt.

Bill Parker, reporting the game for the Associated Press, wrote, "Some women cried over the dramatic finish. Men hollered. Babe smiled, walked off the green—still America's wonder girl athlete and the most promising woman golf player in the United States!"

It pleased Babe Didrikson no end, of course, to read that glowing report in the sports pages, but the match against Mrs. Winger had sobered her considerably. Besides, she was going to meet Peggy Chandler in the finals, and even the exuberant Bill Parker labeled Babe the underdog for that match.

The crowd around the first tee the next afternoon was in the thousands, and, as in all the other matches of the tournament, it was a Babe Didrikson crowd. Americans love an underdog. Americans love a winner. Babe Didrikson was both at the Texas State Women's Golf championship.

Maybe it was the home-crowd kind of support Babe got that inspired her to shoot an eagle 3 on the first of the thirty-six championship holes of the finals. Maybe it was the obvious support of the crowd for Babe that bothered Peggy Chandler and made her bogie the first hole for a 6. Whichever, or both, that was the way it stood as the girls teed off for the second hole.

Before they teed off for the twelfth hole, Babe Didrikson was five up, and she looked like a certain winner.

But just as abruptly, Peggy Chandler began to play beautifully and won the next six holes. At the end of the first eighteen holes of the finals of that Texas championship, the Babe was behind by a stroke. She knew that she had a real battle on her hands.

As for the crowd, their loud cheers for Babe died down as she lost hole after hole.

"It's a beginner against a veteran," they said. "Class and experience will always tell."

There were some who even thought that Babe had folded, that she was finished, that the game was all Chandler's now.

Of course, they were all wrong, wrong on all counts.

Babe came out the next afternoon, for the last eighteen holes of the match, all fired up.

She got a birdie on the first hole.

But so did Peggy Chandler.

Babe was good. But Peggy was better—at least she was better for the first seven of those last eighteen holes. When the two girls teed off for the eighth hole, Peggy was already three up on her challenger.

But on that eighth hole, Babe smacked in a twenty-five-foot putt for a birdie and cut Peggy Chandler's lead to two.

Babe took the ninth hole, too, cutting the lead to one; but Peggy took the next hole to put her two up again.

A determined Babe gave it all she had and, dramatically, she took the eleventh and twelfth holes to tie the match.

The gallery, once again, began to root for the underdog. Babe hadn't folded. The kid was giving the veteran a run for the money.

The two girls split the next three holes.

The sixteenth hole was a par-5.

Peggy Chandler was hitting the ball beautifully. She was right up on the cup for a sure birdie 4. Babe was in trouble with her drive.

Babe's shot off the tee was way in front of Peggy's, but the ball landed in a ditch. Babe took a mighty swing for her second shot, and the ball landed over the green and ran into a roadway. It was a roadway used by trucks, and when Babe found her ball it was in a big, water-filled rut.

Babe knew she couldn't afford to lose this hole.

"I couldn't afford to lose any holes at all," she said, "if I was going to win this championship."

She studied the lie of the ball. Half of the ball was in water. She studied the ground between the ball and the cup on the sixteenth green.

"You can't make any more mistakes, Babe," she said to herself. "Take your time and play this one just right."

She took a sand wedge, the club the great Gene Sarazen had given her.

"Look at the ball real good," she said to herself.

That's a rule no golfer can afford to forget.

She took her stance, looked at the cup, then took her swing, digging the ball out of the rut and sending it toward the pin.

The ball traveled. Babe and everyone else on the grounds had both eyes on the ball as it headed for the cup. And then the roar as the ball sat in the lip of that cup and fell into the hole for an eagle 3.

That one brilliant shot so excited the crowd that they broke all the rules. They roared, broke their lines, and rushed to congratulate Babe; someone actually bowled her over and sent her head down into the mud from which she had shot that ball.

Babe Didrikson was one up on Peggy Chandler, and the crowd just loved it, loved Babe.

Peggy Chandler may have been disheartened by Babe's fantastic shot and by the crowd's open and vigorous rooting for her opponent, but she gave no evidence of it.

She halved the thirty-fifth hole.

There was still the thirty-sixth and final hole, which would decide the championship.

Babe had the match in her hands. She wouldn't let it slip.

Peggy Chandler shot a par for that last hole. Babe birdied the hole to win the championship.

The crowd was ready to carry her off the field in triumph.

It was a great triumph for Babe Didrikson, but she saw it only as a beginning. She was going to enter all the big women's tournaments around the country. She had already entered the Southern Women's Amateur Golf tournament at Louisville, Kentucky, scheduled for May 20.

"I was ready," she said, "to shoot for the national championship."

The newspapers, of course, had the story of the Texas championship all over their sports pages. As Babe had said, it was 1932 all over again. Babe Didrikson was once again America's greatest woman athlete.

Grantland Rice came through with a marvelous tribute. In his syndicated column, which was featured in several hundred papers, he wrote:

From the high jump of Olympic fame,
The hurdles and the rest.
The javelin that flashed its flame
On by the record test—
The Texas Babe now shifts the scene
Where slashing drives are far,
Where spoon shots find the distant green
To break the back of par.

But only two days after the Babe's great triumph in Houston, the newspapers reported that the United States Golf Association was looking into Babe Didrikson's amateur status. There were some people, the newspaper reports continued, who claimed that Babe Didrikson was a professional athlete. They charged that she did not belong in amateur golf.

The newspaper items, of course, came as a shock to Babe Didrikson.

Worse was to come.

Just seventeen days after she had won the Texas State Women's Golf championship, the United States Golf Association, after an allegedly full investigation, ruled that Babe Didrikson was a professional athlete and would no longer be permitted to participate in any amateur women's golf tournament, anywhere in the country, or abroad.

Some people might have been utterly destroyed by such a ruling. Not Babe. Like a good fighter, she could pick herself up from the canvas and come back to win.

# Chapter 11

BABE DIDRIKSON had played professional baseball and professional basketball. Unquestionably she had capitalized on track and field records, and on her Olympic records, in a variety of public appearances for which she had been well paid. But she had never played golf professionally.

Evidently, however, this didn't matter.

"Anyone who pitches, or plays third base for the House of David is a professional," clamored a host of Texas women golfers, among others, and perhaps they were right.

But a lot of other golfers, men mostly, and a good number of sportswriters, telephoned, wrote, or wired their protest of the United States Golf Association's decision that banned Babe from the amateur golf competition.

The great golfer Jimmy Demaret called the United States Golf Association's decision "the biggest joke of the year."

Jack Burke was sharper.

"The dirtiest deal I've heard of," he said.

The president of the Beaumont Country Club, Ben S. Woodhead, called on the Association to give Babe a full hearing.

The United States Golf Association wasn't going to be moved.

"It's for the best interest of the game," they said about

their decision declaring Babe ineligible to participate in any amateur golf tournament.

And that is all they would say.

They never confronted Babe with any charges, and they never gave her an opportunity to clear herself of any charges.

The only way Babe could lift that USGA decision, reverse it, was by way of a rather curious paragraph in the Association's book of rules. The USGA will return the amateur standing to a golfer if that golfer participates in nothing of a professional nature for a period of three years.

Babe was apprised of this peculiar law and gave it some thought. There was no doubt about her desire to continue in amateur golf competition. The big question was money. The $300 a month she was getting for her job with Employers Casualty wasn't nearly enough to keep her going, not when she was still sending so much of what she earned to her family.

Still, she might have taken that three-year hiatus if it weren't for the offers and business propositions that suddenly began to flood in on her.

P. Goldsmith Sons, a sporting-goods company, offered her a retainer of $2,500 a year for letting them use her name on a line of women's golf clubs. P. Goldsmith Sons was later to merge with the MacGregor Golf Company. This was the best commercial offer she had, and she took it.

She was also offered a series of bookings with Gene Sarazen, the top golfer of the day. They were to travel around as a twosome, playing other twosomes around the country. It was too good a proposition for Babe to turn down.

Babe, of course, wasn't in a class with Gene Sarazen, but

her drives were always spectacular and, as the Babe said, "I could give those galleries some good laughs."

Babe Didrikson was always a talker, in any kind of game she played. Playing with Gene Sarazen, she suddenly realized that she had something of the comedian in her makeup.

She would kid Gene Sarazen.

After a long drive she would turn to him and say, "Don't you men wish you could hit the ball like that?"

She would kid herself.

Finding her ball in a clump of bushes, in an impossible lie, she would say, "That was a great shot, wasn't it?"

And she would kid the gallery.

"You all come closer," she would say. "You've heard of Walter Hagen. You've heard of Ben Hogan. But today you're looking at the best."

In any case, just as today's sports fans love the clowning of Muhammad Ali, so did the fans love the jawing of Babe Didrikson.

And Babe was as happy as she had ever been. She was getting that retainer of $2,500 from Goldsmith. She was collecting $500 for each of her appearances on the golf course with Gene Sarazen. She earned enough money to send home to Mamma and Papa in Beaumont, and just as important she was back in the limelight, making the headlines in sports pages once again.

"Didrikson Panics 'Em at Beverly"

"Babe Didrikson outdrives Gene Sarazen"

"It was all 1932 again," as Babe was fond of saying. Nothing had changed except the playing field.

And Babe, too, though she didn't like to admit it, was changing as well. She had grown up, matured, and now with her great success she took on poise and confidence, and her looks changed.

She allowed her hair to grow. It was stylishly waved. She was using a bit of lipstick and a touch of rouge. She was always attractively dressed in well-becoming sports ensembles, and her bag, with her initials on it, matched.

The tomboy look, except for her occasional sharp tongue, had vanished. With the rouge and lipstick in her purse, there was a comb, and a tiny lace handkerchief.

Queried by Paul Gallico once, on her attire, Babe laughed and said, "Yeah, and I've got silk on underneath. And I like it!"

Westbrook Pegler, whose columns in the newspapers across the nation usually reeked of acid, wrote of her at that time, "Babe probably did not realize it but she was a beautiful woman—from the mouth down. I certainly don't mean to be unkind in saying this because I do admire the girl for qualities apart from her skill in all sports. They are determination, courage, honesty, and a candid but not immodest appreciation of her own superiority. Her body is slender but shapely and her legs are beautiful."

The acerbic columnist was not alone in his admiration of the character and the beauty of Babe Didrikson.

She had been a rough-and-tough tomboy growing up in Beaumont, but that didn't mean she wasn't interested in boys. She had dated often enough when she went to Dallas. She remembered two of the men particularly. They had battled each other to become her steady boyfriend, which had amused her no end. She had gone out with one of them more than the other, but she had treated neither of them as a serious suitor, though one young fellow had pressed her to marry him.

"I was too busy working on my career," she said. "I never gave marriage more than a second thought, if I thought of it at all."

When Babe was playing with the House of David baseball team, there was a rumor that she was married, or was about to be married. The story appeared in a column that was syndicated and printed in newspapers all over the country.

Babe neither denied nor confirmed the story.

In a letter to her closest friends in Beaumont, she wrote, "This newspaperman may be right, but I'm not saying a thing. I may be married, but if so it isn't to one of the whisker boys. I'll guarantee you that."

By the "whisker boys" she meant, of course, the House of David.

There were, however, a couple of men Babe might have married, early in her career. There was an All-American six-foot, four-inch football player. There was at least one of the men who managed her.

Nothing came of those episodes either.

As for swingers, Tiny Scurlock once wrote of the Babe, "She had no use for sheiks and they soon learned that she had no use for them. They fell away fast."

When love finally did come to Babe, as it had to in the course of time, it came abruptly. And even then it took some urging and perhaps an ultimatum before she would consider marriage.

That marriage, incidentally, was not only going to please a whole host of her friends, it also was going to please a host of women athletes, friendly and inimical both, around the world.

Until comparatively recently, women had a pretty hard

time of it in athletic competition, any kind of athletic competition. At best, the men looked upon women athletes as oddballs, freaks of nature. And there were enough women who supported their point of view.

The Women's Division of the National Amateur Athletic Federation, which initially had as its motto "a team for everyone and everyone on a team," within six years of its foundation opposed the participation of women in the Olympic Games.

Women physical-education teachers caught up with a phrase Paul Gallico used when he was writing about women athletes as "muscle molls."

"Don't Be a Muscle Moll" was the familiar sign on their bulletin boards.

"My mother cried when I played softball," says Dr. Belle Mead, dean of women's physical education at Lamar University. "I just don't want you to grow up to be like Babe Didrikson."

But the men were best at this job of belittling women athletes.

Paul Gallico described them as "women who made possible deliciously frank and biological discussions as to whether this or that woman athlete should be addressed as Miss, Mrs., Mr., or It."

This was in the days before "Ms." became the popular address it is today.

Joe Williams, the celebrated columnist of the now defunct New York *World-Telegram*, shot his barbs directly at Babe.

"The same year she became the greatest woman athlete in history," he wrote, "a comparative chart showed that she had not equaled one record made by a masculine high school champion of the same period. If the best woman athlete in the country is not as good as some gawky kid in high school, why waste the effort?"

That was bad enough, but not for the acid pen of Joe Williams.

"Why invite the embarrassment of mediocrity?" he added.

Well, Babe was no mediocrity. As for being a woman, Betty Hicks, the fabulous woman golfer, had some words about that. "To those of us who shared the country club locker rooms with her, Babe was conclusively female. She was not feminine by our culture's peculiarly warped definition of it, though she did acquire certain layers of the veneer of femininity. She painted her fingernails, curled her hair, put on high heels, and wore lace-trimmed dresses."

Of course, she continued to act tough, and sometimes crude. It was all part of an act, the kind of act that is great for drawing big crowds, for building gate receipts, adding color to an event; and Babe was in the business of building big crowds for any event in which she participated. In this division of sports, she was considerably ahead of her competitors.

All this was common knowledge, particularly among her fellow women athletes. Still, it was something of a relief for them to observe the change in Babe's looks and her obvious feminine dress.

There was a silent but heartfelt cry of joy among her women confreres when Babe Didrikson announced that she was going steady and would be married.

# Chapter 12

THEODORE VETOYANIS was an American-born son of immigrants who had left Greece for America and settled in Pueblo, Colorado. Theodore's father at first had found work for himself in the steel mills, but then bought a farm just outside the city to work the land he grew to love so much.

Theodore worked on his father's farm and in the steel mills, but he moved on to live with an uncle who had a hat-cleaning shop in Oklahoma City. Here the young man, still in his teens, learned the hat-cleaning business, and shined shoes as well.

Theodore was a big, strong young man, and neither the cleaning of hats nor the shining of shoes could hold him long. Like most young Greeks, and the children of Greeks, for as long as he could remember, he loved to wrestle. Jim Londos, a Greek, was, at that time, the heavyweight wrestling champion of the world.

When Theodore saw an opportunity to enter the ring, as a wrestler, he grabbed it.

It wasn't an easy row he had chosen to hoe for himself, but he was good. He experienced the usual difficulties of a youngster trying to break into the game, but he made it, and he made it big.

He changed his name to George Zaharias. It was a better

name than Vetoyanis for a professional wrestler, and he became one of the top drawing cards in the sport.

One sportswriter dubbed him "The Crying Greek from Cripple Creek," and the name stuck. It was catchy enough for promoters to promote it.

Cripple Creek is a town not too far away from Pueblo, the birthplace of Zaharias. The "Greek" in the nickname was obvious enough. The "Crying" part of it came from the manner in which the wrestler reacted to some of the referee's decisions. George would stand at the edge of the ring, pull on the ropes, and wail loudly enough for everyone in the arena or stadium to hear him. It was all, of course, part of the act that wrestling fans loved. George played his part very well. He was also one of the stage villains the wrestling fans must have, and he played that part well, too. The fans came out in droves to see "The Crying Greek from Cripple Creek" get beaten.

Actually, George Zaharias was neither a cryer nor a villain. Away from the wrestling arena he was really a gentle man, except, some of his best friends would say, when he was involved in a business transaction. When George was involved in a business deal, he could be as hard and as sharp as a Wall Street broker.

When he wasn't involved in a wrestling match, George loved golf. He wasn't a top pro, but he was better than the average player.

It was on a golf course that George Zaharias and Babe Didrikson first met. For all purposes, it was love at first sight.

It was in January of 1938. Babe sent in her entry fee for the Los Angeles Open tournament. The Los Angeles Open was one of the regular tournaments on the men golfers' circuit, but there were no rules barring women from the tournament play.

Babe didn't expect to win it, but she wanted to match her shots against a top men's golfer.

The Babe and one other woman, the great Alice Bauer, were the only women golfers to make the qualifying round. It was no mean accomplishment for Babe at that time of her career.

At the opening round of the tournament itself, she met the two men who were going to play along with her. They were complete strangers. One was C. Pardee Erdman, a Presbyterian minister and professor of religion. The other was husky, black-haired, handsome, 225-pound George Zaharias.

She didn't know who George was, but the sportswriters did, and they could recognize a good picture, as well as a good story, when they saw it.

Before Babe could fully realize what was happening, the photographers were snapping pictures of her in the arms of Zaharias—that is, they were calling on George to put a half nelson on Babe.

"Show us the headlock, George!"

"Now the toehold!"

And George was very happy to oblige, as the crowd around the tee grew larger and larger and the cameras went click!

"The half nelson once again, George!"

It was great fun for George Zaharias. It was almost as much fun for the gallery.

As for Babe, "I didn't mind it at all," she said, smiling broadly.

They drove off the first tee. Something she couldn't explain at the moment kept turning Babe's eyes back to George. George had also been attracted by the clean wholesomeness of Babe Didrikson and he kept his eyes on her. Jack Singer, a Los Angeles newspaperman, had a good idea of what was happening, and he put it very well in his newspaper column.

"The only person in the gallery who was certain of what was going on," he wrote, "was Mrs. Edgar Richards. Now there's one woman who knows what the score is. She ought to. She was the scorekeeper.

"I guess religion still pays," went on the writer, "because the professor finished with a 75. Zaharias finished with 83, the Babe finished with 84, and Mrs. Richards finished with writer's cramp."

Babe enjoyed that writeup as much as the next person. She knew that her mind had not been on the game.

Something was brewing between George Zaharias and Babe Didrikson, and Babe knew that as well.

After the second round, in which both Babe and Zaharias were eliminated, George invited Babe to join him and his brothers, Tom and Chris, for dinner.

The next day they met at the golf course to watch the third round of the tournament.

George asked Babe whether she'd like to go dancing. She asked him to pick her up at home.

Babe was living with her mother and her sister Lillie near the Paramount Studios at the time.

Lillie remembers that Babe asked her to comb her hair before George arrived.

George remembers Mamma Didrikson patting him on the cheek and saying, "My Babe likes you."

Babe and George went dancing at the Cotton Club. The club artist drew a charcoal sketch of each of them.

George autographed his picture and gave it to Babe.

Babe autographed her picture and gave it to George.

It was a real storybook romance. But it was not a passing thing. It was a romance that was going to last for the rest of Babe Didrikson's life.

"Romance," he called her.

And she called him "Romance."

That was the way they would greet each other. That is the way they would sign notes and letters to each other.

Babe didn't go to the wrestling matches to see her George wrestle.

"She didn't like the bouts because she thought I might get hurt," said George.

But George was always searching for, and finding, Babe at some driving range.

They were now inseparable, and all the gossip columnists had a field day with the love affair between George and Babe.

Finally the time came when Mamma Didrikson had to go home to Beaumont, and Babe had to drive her there with Lillie. George had to wrestle around California, and the couple had to separate.

It was a tough ride for Babe.

"The farther we got away from Los Angeles," said Babe, "the more I missed him. I was feeling really bad."

When she stopped in Phoenix, so that Mamma Didrikson could visit with Babe's older sister Dora, Babe was utterly miserable.

"Mamma," she said, "would you mind taking the train back to Beaumont?"

Mamma Didrikson was very understanding.

"I'll take the train back to Beaumont," she said. "Don't worry. Lillie will be with me."

She looked at her daughter lovingly.

"You go back to George," she said. "He misses you, too."

Babe jumped into her car and raced the 389 miles back to Los Angeles.

She pulled up in front of the apartment in which George lived. She rang the bell. She rang it again. No one was home.

Her face was teary; she had missed him.

But there was a note on the door. She hadn't noticed it in her haste.

"Romance," it began.

The note was for her.

Her heart began to beat more rapidly.

"I'm in San Francisco," read the rest of the love message to her.

Chris, George's brother, opened the door. He had been sleeping.

"I thought you were in Beaumont," he said.

"I'm here," said Babe. "Please drive with me to San Francisco, Chris!"

"Four hundred miles? Now?" asked Chris. "Can't it wait till the morning?"

"No!" said Babe. "Now! I'm leaving now! Do you want to come with me, or don't you?"

They drove through the night.

In the morning, just after dawn, they pulled up in front of the St. Marks Hotel, where all the wrestlers stayed.

Babe raced up the stairs and pounded at the door of George's room.

A sleepy George, in his robe, opened the door.

A big smile lit his face.

"Come here, Romance," he said.

They embraced, and Babe, tired and worn, heaved a great sigh. She was with her man again.

There had to be ·moments when they were apart. They each had separate professional commitments. However, George tried to arrange his wrestling dates so that they would always be near to where Babe was playing golf.

Babe entered the Western Women's Open golf tournament in June of that year. That year the tournament was to be held in Colorado Springs. Colorado Springs is not too far from Pueblo, and George had Babe out to meet his family. It was all very loving and comforting.

Babe was eliminated in the semifinal round of the Women's Open, but it didn't matter much to her. Nothing really mattered much to her then but George.

They drove together to St. Louis, where George was wrestling. Babe had to make a quick trip to Cincinnati, to the headquarters of the sporting-goods people who were still paying her $2,500 a year, but she was back in St. Louis in a hurry.

On July 22 of that year, just six months after they had first met, Babe and George announced their engagement. They began to plan for their wedding.

Setting the date, however, proved more difficult than they had expected. Babe was always off on some exhibition. George had a wrestling match in some other town, or he had to attend to one of his many business deals, his clothing shops, his pro football team (the San Diego Gunners), his hotel in Denver.

They kept postponing and postponing the day for their

marriage until George Zaharias couldn't take it any more. That is when he delivered his ultimatum.

"We're going to get married this week," he said to Babe, with no little passion, "or we call the deal off!"

"The deal's on," said Babe. "We get married this week."

On December 23, 1938, Babe Didrikson became Mrs. George Zaharias.

Baseball star Leo Durocher was at the wedding, with his wife. Home-run star Joe Medwick and his wife were there. Durocher was George's best man. Leo's wife was Babe's matron of honor.

It was a relatively small wedding. It took place in the home of Tom Packs, a wrestling promoter. There wasn't time to invite anyone but their closest St. Louis friends to the ceremony and the small party that followed. But Babe and George were two happy people.

"Honey, I've got you at last," said George.

"No," said Babe. "I've got you."

Well, they certainly had each other, and they were certainly very much in love.

Babe wanted to leave St. Louis right after the wedding ceremony, her mind and heart set on a long honeymoon, with George and herself at last alone, together, and away from all the pressures of golf, wrestling, and their other commitments.

George was just as eager for the freedom of being alone with Babe, with no telephone to answer, no urgent wires demanding urgent replies, no wrestling, no golf, no demands from others on their time.

But it couldn't be. They were both booked through March with contracts they couldn't afford to break. The honeymoon would come. George promised Babe their honeymoon would be the greatest. But it had to wait. It was going to wait till April.

Babe had always dreamed of taking a long boat ride, something like "a slow boat to China."

But China was out at that moment in its history. It was having all the troubles it could handle, battling off the Japanese. Babe forgot about that slow boat to China till that morning in April when George said, very simply, "Get your things packed, honey."

"Where are we going?" asked Babe, almost indifferently.

They were always going off for a wrestling match, on a business deal. But this wasn't one of that kind of trip.

"We're going on a long one this time, honey," said George, still playing the game.

"Florida?" queried Babe, still not excited.

"Longer than that," said George.

"China?" burst out Mrs. George Zaharias.

"No," said George. "You know we can't do that."

"Then where?" pressed Babe. "Let me hear it!"

George smiled.

"We're going to take a slow boat . . ."

"China!" insisted Babe.

"Australia," said George.

"Australia!" repeated Babe, beside herself with a sudden joy. "George!"

She kissed him, hugged him, kissed him again.

"Let's go!" she hollered.

Dreams sometimes come true. At least this was one dream that came true for Babe Didrikson Zaharias.

In fact, that trip to Australia was to prove more beautiful and happier than anything Babe had ever dreamed of.

# Chapter 13

WHEN BABE arrived in Australia she discovered a surprise for her. Archie Keene, an Australian promoter, following the instructions of George Zaharias, had arranged a golf tour for her.

Nothing could have pleased Babe more. She became more and more pleased as she moved from Sydney to Bath, from Bath to Perth, to play an exhibition match in almost all the big cities "down under" and in a score of smaller towns as well.

Wherever she went, there was a huge audience to greet her. At first there was a polite applause to accompany the curiosity of the galleries, and then the cheers of the crowds as Babe demonstrated her tremendous ability on the golf course.

She impressed them all, including the sportswriters, even those who had been skeptical about the feats of the American.

Jack Dillo, an Australian sportswriter who had been perhaps the most skeptical of the lot, found himself writing, "If Miss Didrikson tightens up on her short game, she may get a place among the best men professionals in golf."

He didn't have to be convinced about her ability to drive the ball those phenomenal distances.

Babe played in New Zealand. She played in Honolulu. And always there was the huge gallery and the tremendous welcome and enthusiasm. When they finally got back to the States, as much as she had enjoyed that beautifully long and triumphant journey, Babe was a little dispirited.

"Where do we go from here, George?" she asked.

It was obvious that there wasn't much room for a woman playing pro golf in America, at that time. There were very few professional women golfers in that era, and the competition in the field was severely limited.

Babe and George ticked off the names of all the scheduled tournaments in which Babe could enter.

"I can't play in this one. I can't play in that one," said Babe. "I'm a professional," she complained. "There's almost nowhere I can play."

"You could become an amateur again," suggested George.

"That means I'll have to cancel all my contracts," said Babe. "I won't be able to make all those public appearances."

"Not for a fee," said George. "You could play if you made it plain that you couldn't accept any of the prize money," he added.

"I could do that, couldn't I?" mused the great woman athlete.

"We don't need the money," offered George Zaharias.

That was true enough. George was earning something like $100,000 a year. Money was no longer a problem with Babe. Of course, she would hate to give up any kind of prize money, but that would amount to a very small sacrifice. Besides, she had no other choice if she was to prove how good a golfer she was in competition.

"Three years," said Babe, putting up the last possible argument against her decision. "That's a long time."

The United States Golf Association would require Babe to keep a simon-pure record for that length of time, three years in which she could earn no money at the game, or at anything related to professional sports, like business deals or exhibitions for fee, before they would consider returning her to amateur status.

"It'll be worth it," said George.

And the Babe agreed with him.

She penned her application for reinstatement as an amateur and delivered it to the offices of the United States Golf Association.

The rewards and the wait would be worth the pain.

In the interim, Babe went back to tennis for a while. She took lessons with Eleanor Tennant. Eleanor Tennant had given lessons to Alice Marble and Little Mo Connolly, two of the finest women tennis players of that time.

When she thought she was good enough, Babe took to the tennis courts against Mary Arnold and Louise Brough, two more of the top tennis stars.

Babe played with a number of movie stars who were also good tennis players, men like Errol Flynn, Paul Lukas, Peter Lorre, John Garfield.

"I think you're good enough to play tournament tennis," said Eleanor Tennant after a while.

Babe was sure she was good enough.

She sent in her request to participate in the Pacific Southwest tennis championships, and Babe was full of confidence.

"I don't think I'll win it," she admitted, frankly enough, "but I'll give them a good run for the cup."

Unhappily, Babe was in for a quick letdown. The Pacific Southwest tennis people returned her application.

Babe was a professional, they ruled. She didn't qualify as an amateur. What was worse, the tennis ruling had it that "once a pro, always a pro."

Tennis, abruptly, was out for Babe Didrikson Zaharias.

But she did enter the Western Women's Open golf tournament in 1940, and won the tournament.

She also took the Texas Women's Open in 1940.

The Western and the Texas were the two big women's golf tournaments of the year, and Babe had taken them both for what was called golf's "Little Slam."

Babe found great satisfaction in her showing on the golf course that year, and so did her doting husband.

It compensated, if only a bit, for her disappointment in tennis.

In 1941, Babe played some exhibitions, mostly for the benefit of one charity or another. And then came the great shock of the Japanese sneak attack on Pearl Harbor, the anger, the cry for retaliation, and America's entry into the arenas of World War II.

Both Babe and George, immediately, wanted to enlist in the armed forces of the country. George thought he could teach the Army, the Navy, the Air Corps, the Marines, any or all of them, the art of hand-to-hand fighting—after all, he was one of the leading wrestlers in the world.

But the armed forces turned George down. They all turned him down, much to his great anger. There was nothing, however, he could do about it. He had varicose veins, which made him too much of a risk for any of the services.

Babe didn't find a place with any of women's corps, either.

Instead, she appeared in all sorts of sports exhibition games for the war effort, and for war charities as well.

She appeared in a number of golf matches, and two of her favorite partners in these appearances were the famous singer Bing Crosby and the great comedian Bob Hope.

"Bing was the better player," said Babe. "He was just about the best golfer the movie stars could produce. But Bob Hope," she added, "was funnier."

Of course, Bob Hope supplied all the comedy, or almost all of it, in these exhibitions.

"There's only one thing wrong about Babe and me," was one of his usual lines. "I hit the ball like a girl and she hits like a man."

He clowned all over the greens.

Every time Babe got off one of her long drives, Hope would fall to the ground, beat it with his fists, and let out a long and anguished wail, which would call on Bing to kneel down and comfort the sobbing comic.

Hope would miss a putt, miss a second try at the cup, then, with a flourish he would announce, as he approached a third try at getting the ball into the hole, "This is the same man putting."

Babe had a line herself that she contributed to the festivities and that would always prove a favorite with the galleries.

She would point to her husband, George, who was generally in the gallery when she played, and loudly declare, so everyone would hear her, "Look at him! When I married him, he was a Greek god. Now he's a big fat Greek."

George was close to three hundred pounds at the time, and getting bigger. Babe's quip was always sure for a big laugh, and George was sport enough to laugh right along with the gallery.

Finally, on January 21, 1943, Babe got the good news from the United States Golf Association. On January 21, 1943, Babe Didrikson Zaharias was once again an amateur golfer.

She wasn't slow getting back into competition.

Her first appearance, as an amateur again, was in a charity exhibition match at the Desert Golf Club in Palm Springs. She played against Clara Callender, the California State women's champion. Babe beat Miss Callender four up, with two holes to play.

She beat Miss Callender again, some ten days later, to take the women's golf championship at the Los Angeles Country Club.

It was one tournament after another after that, and Babe took almost every one of them.

She had won the Western Women's Open in 1940, playing as a professional. She won it as an amateur in 1944, and again in 1945.

The Associated Press poll of American sportswriters and sportscasters said it all, voting Babe Didrikson Zaharias, in 1945, "Woman Athlete of the Year."

"Although Mrs. Zaharias first won fame as a track star," read the Associated Press citation accompanying the award, "and later competed in most sports as an amateur and professional, she now concentrates on golf. It was in that field that she was outstanding during the 1945 campaign.

"In addition to defeating Betty Jameson in a seventy-two-hole challenge match at Los Angeles and San Antonio," continued the citation, "Mrs. Zaharias became the first woman to capture three Western Open golf titles. Although she was upset by Phyllis Otto in the Western Amateur, she bounced back to cop the Texas Open."

This was the third time that Babe had been named "Woman Athlete of the Year" in the annual Associated Press poll of sportswriters and sportscasters. The first time she was voted the honor came after her magnificent triumphs at the 1932 Olympic Games.

She was to win that honor of being declared the greatest woman athlete of the year again and again and again. And, at another time, not too far off, these sportswriters and sportscasters were yet to accord Babe Didrikson Zaharias another and even greater honor.

Babe Didrikson Zaharias had not yet reached the pinnacle of her prowess on the golf course. She was still a few short years away from her most magnificent achievements.

# Chapter 14

BABE WASN'T in top form when the 1946 tournament got under way. She lost, in June, to Mary McMillin in a semifinals match of the Western Women's Amateur tournament. It was the last tournament that Babe Didrikson Zaharias was going to lose in a long, long time.

She beat Polly Riley, on her next outing, in the Trans-Mississippi Women's Amateur in Denver for that women's championship, and she would not be beaten again for years. She was off on a winning streak that has never been equaled by any golfer, man or woman, professional or amateur to this day.

She beat lovely Dorothy Kielty of St. Paul by six and four to win the Broadmoor Invitational Match Play tournament in Colorado Springs. She won George S. May's All-American championship at the Tam O'Shanter Country Club in Niles, Illinois.

That made three straight tournament victories.

She met Clara Callender, once again, in the finals of the National Women's Amateur at the Southern Hills Country Club in Tulsa, Oklahoma, and ran away with the match. The score was eleven up with just nine holes to go, and Babe Didrikson Zaharias had her fourth straight win.

That was the way it was going to go.

She beat Betty Hicks, five and three, to take the Texas Women's Open. She beat Louise Suggs by 5 strokes to win the Tampa Open. She took the Helen Lee Doherty Women's Amateur championship at the Miami Country Club, beating Margaret Gunther by twelve and ten.

People began to whisper that George was Babe's secret weapon. In a way, he was. Babe had never been happier in her life, or more at ease, or more comfortable with herself, and George, in a good measure, was responsible for that. Babe was deeply in love with George, and George, big and broad as he was, was deeply and tenderly in love with Babe. With all that love around her, Babe Didrikson Zaharias couldn't help but be at her best in these tournaments.

But the whispering on and off the golf course was not about their love, but about George's presence on the greens, at the tee, even in the rough, if Babe found herself there. Babe got pretty much fed up with the stories. One day she turned around to the whisperers, and there were a good many reporters among them, and she let them have it.

"See the way the green slants down past the cup," she indicated to the newspapermen and everyone else in the gallery. "Well, the reason George follows me is because he's so heavy that any side of the green he's standing on leans his way."

That one drew a self-conscious laugh from sportswriters and a healthier laugh from the gallery.

There was also talk about George's smoke signals. It was suggested that George sent up the smoke from his cigars so that Babe could better judge the way the wind was blowing on the course.

Babe was a bit angrier about that one.

"If after all these years," she said, "I don't know which way the wind is blowing, I'd better turn in my clubs."

She didn't turn in her clubs.

She just went right on winning tournament after tournament.

Paired with Gerald Walker, she won the Florida Mixed Two-ball championship at Orlando, Florida, to make it eight straight wins.

Down two holes with only three to go, she took those last three to beat Jean Hopkins in the Palm Beach Women's Amateur.

The Women's International Four-ball at Hollywood, Florida, was a close one, but, with Peggy Kirk as her partner, she won beating Louise Suggs and Jean Hopkins for her tenth straight tournament win.

She beat Peggy Kirk for the South Atlantic Women's championship in Ormond Beach. She won the Florida East Coast Women's championship at St. Augustine, beating Mary Agnes Wall. At one moment in the Women's Title-holders tournament at Augusta, Georgia, Babe found herself 10 strokes behind Dorothy Kirby, but she came back to take the tournament by 5 strokes for her thirteenth straight victory.

It took two holes of sudden-death play in the North and South Amateur in Pinehurst, North Carolina, but Louise Suggs proved the victim in Babe's fourteenth straight win. The fifteenth straight tournament victory for Babe came in the women's division of the Celebrities tournament in Washington, D.C. It was an incredible victory streak, but the constant travel and tense nerve-wracking competition were getting to Babe. She wanted to go home for a long, well-earned rest. It simply wasn't in the cards.

"Do you think Babe should go to Scotland?" George Zaharias, always ambitious for Babe's career, asked Tommy Armour, an all-time great golfer.

They had been sitting around, just the three of them, Babe, George, and Armour.

"Do you think she ought to go out for the British Women's Amateur?"

No American woman had ever taken that title, though a good number had tried.

"I think so," said Tommy, himself a Scot.

"I don't know," said Babe. "It's a long trip. Would you go with me, George?"

"Of course I'll go with you," George responded quickly. "If I can get away, I'll go with you."

"I know what that means," said Babe. "I'd have to go alone, and I'm not sure I'd like that."

It was Tommy Armour's turn to talk.

"Mildred," he said. He always called Babe "Mildred." "Whether George can go or not, you go!"

Again and again and again, Babe would be reminded that no woman had ever brought the British Women's Amateur cup back to America. Bobby Jones, Ben Hogan, Gene Sarazen, Sam Snead, Walter Hagen, all the greatest among golfers, and all Americans, had brought the British Men's Amateur championship back home with them. But the greatest women golfers who had tried for the British Women's Amateur had all come home empty-handed.

It was a great challenge for Babe Didrikson Zaharias. What was more, Babe knew that winning the British Women's Amateur would establish her firmly as the greatest woman golfer in the entire world. It was a prize she had long desired. It was a prize for which, she knew, ultimately, she must aim. It was a prize she could not deny herself.

Babe went.

As she had suspected, George was completely tied up in all his business wheeling and dealing.

She went alone.

She was to be a stranger in a strange land, but she wasn't terribly afraid of that. She had always gotten along with people. She knew that she was going to miss George. What she didn't know was how kind, courteous, and friendly both the Scots and the English were going to be to her.

The British Women's Amateur, in 1947, was played on the Gullane golf course, some thirty-five miles out of Scotland's capital city, Edinburgh. Babe stayed at the North Berwick Inn, within walking distance of the course, where they went all-out to make her comfortable.

The townspeople made her feel comfortable, too, with their "Good morning, Mrs. Zaharias" and their "Good afternoon, Mrs. Zaharias" and their "Good evening, Mrs. Zaharias."

Mrs. Zaharias asked the newspapermen whether they couldn't get those kind folks to call her Babe. After which some, but not many, did. The Scots are a very polite people. The course came as a bit of a surprise to Babe. The grounds were not kept quite as neat and as private as the American golf courses. On Sundays, when there is no golf in church-minded Scotland, people just wandered over the greens and set themselves down for picnics. Sunday or any other day in the week, even when there were golfers on the course, there were sheep moving around, chewing on the grass.

Babe got used to that quickly enough. The sheep were wise enough to get out of the way of the golfers, when they had to. But she found the galleries that followed the players a bit odd.

In England and Scotland the galleries are exceptionally quiet. They don't applaud, until perhaps at the end of a match. They don't shout and yell and stampede, as they often do in the States. At most, some one or another of the spectators might utter a very quiet, "Well played," or "Good shot."

Babe would change all that—a little, but not too much.

There were ninety-nine of the finest women golfers in the world entered in the tournament for the British Women's Amateur championship. The schedule called for an eighteen-hole match in the morning, and another, if one survived, in the afternoon. The two women who would oppose each other in the finals would play thirty-six holes for the championship—eighteen in the morning, eighteen in the afternoon.

Babe was in top form as the tournament began. She clinched the first match, against Helen Nimmo, at the twelfth hole.

"Gee," Babe thought to herself as she won hole after hole without any recognition from the gallery, "you have to knock the ball in the hole off the tee to get any applause around here."

The gallery did applaud with some little enthusiasm when Babe came home a winner in her first match of the tournament.

In the afternoon, she pleaded with the gallery to loosen up.

"Come on," she called out to them, "let's have some fun."

The gallery smiled, amused by this strange American. But

again, it was just the polite applause as she took her second round, four and two, from Mrs. Enid Sheppard.

At the end of that round, Babe Didrikson Zaharias treated the gallery to some of her trick shots, the kind of shots with which she entertained at exhibitions back home.

She put a kitchen match behind her ball on the tee and teed off for the eighteenth hole. The match popped off with the bang of a small cannon.

That little trick stirred up the crowd.

In a trap, she put one ball on top of the other, then took her swing. The trick was to get one ball on the green, the other in her pocket. This time the ball went into her pocket, all right, and the other ball right into the cup.

That fancy little trick startled the gallery, and they applauded.

She had one more trick to show them that afternoon. She putted the ball between her legs, sending the ball into the cup; and that one finally got the crowd into an uproar.

Next day, Babe won her morning and afternoon matches again. In the morning she beat Mrs. Val Reddan five and four. In the afternoon she took Mrs. Cosmo Falconer six and five.

She was getting the newspaper headlines again.

### "Our Girls Shaken by Golf Babe"

Fred Pignon, a noted British sportswriter wrote, "Mrs. Zaharias crashed her way over the hills and dales of this testing, undulating course. She tore holes in the rough with tremendous recovery shots and simply battered her opponents in both her matches with the most tremendous exhibition of long driving ever seen in women's golf."

Against Frances Stephens, in the quarterfinals, Babe

found the opposition a bit tougher, but she emerged the winner, three and two. That afternoon she was to play against one of the tournament's favorites, Jean Donald, and the crowds at Gullane were up for it. As the Associated Press story ran, "The crowd, attracted by the report that the Scottish champion was out to slay the American champion, grew to almost unmanageable proportions."

The British have a quaint way of putting things.

"Estimated by golf writers at between five thousand and eight thousand," went on the Associated Press report, "the gallery was the largest of the season, far larger than the crowd which gathered to watch the British Men's Amateur at Carnoustie two weeks previously. Nearly one hundred police barely preserved order."

Babe Didrikson Zaharias drew the crowds wherever she went.

The Scottish champion was no match for Babe that afternoon. The match came as almost a sad anticlimax after all the ballyhoo. Babe was six up at the twelfth hole. She put away the match at the thirteenth. Babe was in the finals. Her opponent was a very fine woman golfer, Jacqueline Gordon.

Babe dressed beautifully for this important last day of the tournament. She came to the course dressed in a neat gray flannel skirt, a wool sweater over her yellow-and-white blouse.

In a gesture of good will, she saluted a flying Union Jack, the flag of Great Britain; then, in her typically theatrical manner, she salaamed three times to the Star-Spangled Banner the Scots had raised on a flagpole.

The crowd—and it was a big one again—applauded her salute to the Union Jack. They roared when she paid her homage to the Stars and Stripes.

Then came the serious business of the match against Jacqueline Gordon.

Miss Gordon, a top-notch golfer, could drive that ball almost as well as the Babe. She had to win her way to the British Women's finals. At the twelfth hole of the morning's play, she was two up on Babe Didrikson Zaharias. Babe struggled to bring the match to a standoff at the eighteenth hole.

In the afternoon, for the final eighteen holes of the tournament for the championship, it was quite a different story.

"My lucky pants did it," Babe would say later.

In any case, following the morning session on the course, she hurried back to her inn for some lunch and, more important, a change of clothes. She needed to wear something warmer for the chilly Scot weather, and part of that change involved getting into her siren suit and those "lucky pants."

Actually, Babe wasn't given to being superstitious. It had been the press who had dubbed her slacks as her "lucky pants." Whatever the case, Babe came out strong for those last eighteen holes of the tournament, determined to take the championship.

For a while Jacqueline Gordon held her own. But not for long. Babe was simply superb and, as the two women approached the back nine holes, Babe Didrikson Zaharias was five up on her opponent.

Jacqueline Gordon did take the tenth hole to cut Babe's lead to four up, but it was the only hole she won in the entire match. Babe got back her five up lead at the eleventh hole and, at the fourteenth, it was all over. Babe Didrikson Zaharias was the winner, the British Women's Amateur champion, the *first American woman* to win that coveted prize, and the crowd finally broke loose and gave Babe the most tremendously warm and enthusiastic ovation the Scot course had ever witnessed.

"Surely no woman golfer has accomplished in a championship what Mrs. Zaharias achieved in this one," wrote an astounded and admiring sportswriter for the English Manchester *Guardian*.

"She has combined in a remarkable way immense length with accuracy," continued the writer, as if he couldn't quite believe what he had seen. "She is a crushing and heartbreaking opponent."

It was a great triumph.

George was waiting for her as she came home on the *Queen Elizabeth*. He came out on a tugboat that was jammed with newspapermen and cameramen eager to interview the homecoming champion, eager to photograph her.

"Watch out, honey!" she yelled to her husband as he stepped on board the ocean liner. "You're turning the boat over!"

There was a parade through the entire city of Denver, Babe's hometown at the time. There were floats for each of the sports or events in which she had starred, basketball, javelin, hurdles, golf of course, and even baseball. Babe rode in the last float, heaped with roses, throwing those roses to the huge crowd of more than fifty thousand persons who lined the streets of Denver to greet her and to pay homage to their heroine.

Babe Didrikson Zaharias was at last acknowledged as the greatest woman golfer in the world. She knew it. And she reveled in it.

# Chapter 15

THERE WAS one more tournament for Babe Didrikson Zaharias, in 1947. It was the Broadmoor Match-play tournament in Colorado Springs, and she took that tournament, beating lovely Dot Kielty in the finals, ten and nine.

This was the seventeenth straight win for Babe in that streak of victories that "has never been" equaled.

She had been voted "Woman Athlete of the Year," for the third time, by the Associated Press poll of sportswriters and sportscasters, in 1946.

They voted her "Woman Athlete of the Year" for the fourth time, in 1947.

Now Babe was bombarded with commercial offers, among them an offer to do ten short golf films for the tidy sum of $300,000.

She certainly didn't need the money, but a deal like that wasn't to be turned down too easily.

Babe talked it over with George.

George, always the promoter, thought the time was just about right to organize a women's pro golf tour. He thought that Babe had created sufficient interest in women's golf to make it a paying proposition.

"I hate to give up my amateur standing," said Babe. "We've worked so hard to get it," she added, including George in the struggle.

"It's up to you, honey," said George. "Anything you want will be O.K. with me."

It didn't take Babe too long to decide.

On August 14, 1947, she called a press conference in New York.

"I'm turning pro," she announced simply.

The newspapermen weren't surprised. They knew what an attraction Babe was, and the kind of gate she could draw. They also thought that she had well earned the kind of money she was sure to make as a professional.

"Fred Corcoran is my business agent," she said.

Fred Corcoran represented some of the top people in sports. Ted Williams, the Boston slugger, and Stan the Man Musial of the St. Louis Cardinals were among his clients.

George Zaharias would give up his wrestling career and almost all his other business activities to manage her interests.

Her past had been bright enough. The future looked even brighter for Babe Didrikson Zaharias.

The big $300,000 movie deal fell through, but Babe did make three movie shorts for Columbia Pictures.

Wilson Sporting Goods Company signed her on as a member of their advisory staff. They also gave her a contract for a line of Babe Zaharias golf equipment.

Lou Serbin, one of the nation's leading dress designers located in Miami, signed for a line of golf dresses, to be designed by Babe.

Fred Corcoran, always with George Zaharias' approval, arranged a number of exhibitions for Babe, some of them as before-game attractions in the big-league baseball parks.

Before a Yankee game, she got Joe DiMaggio to the plate, to pitch to him.

Joe, always shy, demurred, but Babe practically dragged him out of the dugout.

"Come on, Joe!" And then, once he started to pump his bat, she called out to him, with reasonable fear, "Now don't you line one back at me!"

DiMaggio may have smiled. Sometimes his smile was so faint that it was hard to find.

Then Joe sent a few long fouls into the stands. And finally, perhaps to please the fans, perhaps to please Babe, or because Babe was that good, no one knows which, he took a good cut and missed, for strike three, and out.

Joe didn't run, but he got back to his dugout quickly enough.

At another of these pre-game exhibitions, she took on the slugging Ted Williams in a driving match.

"Most of my shots went farther than his," said Babe, "but I'll have to admit that he whaled some of them a distance I've never gotten on any of my tee shots."

At one time or another Babe appeared in golf exhibitions with any number of the sports world's greats, or appeared with them at some public function. And most of them remained her friends for the rest of her life. She was an outgoing person, loved company, loved laughs.

She played with Babe Ruth in a charity golf exhibition. She was with Jim Thorpe and Danny Kaye, that great comedian, at the Los Angeles Celebrity tournament. She was with former Heavyweight Champion Jack Sharkey at a Sportsman's Show. She joined the great Joe Louis in another of her exhibition golf tourneys. She played golf with Spencer Tracy and showed Katharine Hepburn how to swing her various golf clubs. Of course, Babe knew, or would know, all the top greats in golf—Bobby Jones, Cary Middlecoff, Sam Snead, and the rest; and she even gave President Eisenhower tips on how to improve his game.

Babe was a woman almost everybody, except perhaps some of her women competitors, loved to have around. And even most of those women who competed against her came to love her.

"Babe was the great athlete I'll never be," said Patty Berg, an outstanding golf champion in her own right. "She just had a tremendous amount of color, but she was easy to be with. She was a beautiful lady and a wonderful friend."

In 1948 Babe took on a nerve-wracking schedule that Fred Corcoran had booked for her. At one period during that stretch—one month, to be exact—she spent seventeen nights traveling by plane from one city to another. It was a grueling pace.

Still, she made an effort to enter the men's National Open championship.

She didn't make it, much as she would have liked to see how well she could do in competition with the other sex.

The United States Golf Association seemed to be embarrassed, turning down Babe's application. They issued a statement to the press to explain their position.

"As the championship has always been intended to be for men, the eligibility rules have been rephrased to confirm that condition. Thus, the USGA has declined an informal entry submitted in behalf of Mrs. George Zaharias."

Babe was amused by the need of the USGA to "rephrase" their laws, but she was realistic, evaluating her chances in such a tournament.

"I don't suppose I'd have finished around the top," she said. "But I wouldn't have disgraced myself, either."

Babe did play, however, in the first National Women's Open at the Atlantic City Country Club, and took $1,200 as first-prize money.

Altogether, Babe won $3,400 that year in golf competition, and she was the leading money-winner at that. There wasn't very much, by way of cash prizes, for professional women golfers in 1948.

George Zaharias came up with an idea to remedy that situation.

Actually, George had first promoted the idea, when all those commercial offers began to come in for the Babe, after her triumph in the British Women's Amateur tournament. He began to put the idea to work late in 1948.

There were very few professional women golfers to organize at that time. There were Patty Berg, Helen Dettweiler, Bea Gottlieb, Betty Hicks, and Betty Jameson, to list them alphabetically. There were a couple of others and, of course, there was Babe Didrikson Zaharias.

It was indeed a small group of professionals, but it was an impressive group. It certainly was a fine nucleus to begin with, and George Zaharias promoted it.

He got the Wilson Sporting Goods Company to put up some money, and he got Fred Corcoran to do the organizational work necessary. Shortly after New Year's Day, in January of 1949, Fred Corcoran, George Zaharias, Patty Berg, and Babe held a meeting at the Venetian Hotel in Miami. It was here that the Ladies' Professional Golf Association was born.

Hope Seignious had been president of a practically defunct Women's Professional Golf Association. They called Hope, from Miami, and invited her to take the post of president of the new organization.

Hope Seignious thanked them for the honor but pleaded that she was too ill to take on the responsibility.

"You'll have all the support I can give you, however," she added. "And I do wish you luck!"

Patty Berg was elected the first president of the newborn Ladies' Professional Golf Association.

The LPGA was a brave venture, destined to succeed, and succeed fast.

In 1949, the total purses in the Ladies' Professional Golf Association came to some $15,000. By 1955, the last year in which Babe would play, the minimum purse was $5,000 for a tournament. The total prize money for the year came to about $200,000. Even allowing for inflation, which wasn't what it is today, the LPGA had gone a long way in six short years. Thanks to the promotional energy of George Zaharias, the organizational ability of Fred Corcoran, the support of Wilson Sporting Goods Company, and especially the brilliance of America's women golfers, women's professional golf had at last come to be respected for the game it is, an integral part of the great American sports scene.

And, of course, it was the great playing of Babe Didrikson Zaharias, the color and drama she brought to the game, that was to provide the dynamic impetus to this development. In more ways than one, one may consider the Ladies' Professional Golf Association as a living monument to that greatest of America's women athletes, living or gone.

# Chapter 16

FROM ITS inception, Babe Didrikson Zaharias was the queen of women's professional golf. She would be the queen until the untimely day of her death. Louise Suggs, Patty Berg, and Betty Jameson were all former U.S. amateur champions. All three had won the U. S. Women's Open. Each one of them was capable of beating Babe on the links on any given day. But Babe was to remain the star. She was to remain the biggest money-winner on the women's professional circuit. She would continue to be the biggest woman attraction on the golf course. That last is a bit of an understatement. There were few golfers, men or women, who could draw the crowds the Babe did.

And it was Babe who was largely responsible for changing the life-style of the women pro golfers, Betty Hicks, Helen Dettweiler, Katherine Hemphill, Mary Mozel, Opal Hill, Sally Sessions, Shirley Mueller, Bea Gottlieb, the Bauer sisters, and the rest.

Now there was a sudden rash of offers from sporting-goods stores, with lucrative contracts, for the girls. Golf clubs began to call on them to become resident pros. Babe was lured to Grossinger's world-famous resort in New York's Catskill Mountains for a fancy fee. The girls no longer had to find some friend to house them during a tournament. Famous resorts like Grossinger's began to provide them with elegant suites, for the privilege of entertaining them. And they were all parking their own cars, some of them gifts from automobile companies eager for the publicity they could get out of it.

Babe drove a Cadillac convertible with the name "Babe" lettered brightly and broadly on the doors.

The year 1948 was the dawn of a new and a great era for women professional golfers. For Babe Didrikson, from 1948 to almost the end of her days, it was the beginning of a Roman holiday.

She won the All-American tournament, the World championship, and the National Open in 1948. She was tied in the Augusta Titleholders tournament and runner-up in the Texas Open, the Western Open, and the Hardcastle Open.

In 1949, Babe took the Eastern Open and, for the second time, the World championship.

The year 1950 proved to be a big one for the Babe. She was the winner of the Augusta Titleholder tournament, the 144-hole Weathervane tournament, the Western Open, the All-American championship, the National Open and, for the third straight time, the World championship.

This was the year that the Associated Press poll of sportswriters and sportscasters voted Babe Didrikson Zaharias the "World's Greatest Woman Athlete of the First Half of the Twentieth Century."

The Babe wore her honors well. She was just a bit more of a lady in her deportment than she had been when she was a track and field star, a basketball player, a young golfer, but she was still the rough-and-tumble, hail-fellow-well-met, exuberant woman she would always be. And her husband,

George Zaharias, was always along to keep her company and to remind her of her less affluent days.

Babe was offered a job, in 1950, at the Sky Crest Country Club, as the club's teaching pro. It was an offer she couldn't refuse. The Sky Crest, located just outside Chicago, guaranteed her $20,000 a year, with no limit on any of the exhibitions she wished to make or the tournaments she wished to play.

The Sky Crest Country Club, of course, put her up in elegant quarters and, as Babe put it, she and George "were really living high off the hog."

One night, on the way to the Sky Crest, George pulled their car up in front of a diner. They walked in, sat on two stools at the counter, and George ordered.

"Two hamburgers, two bowls of chili, and two glasses of buttermilk."

Babe gave George one of those quizzical looks. They had been eating nothing but choice, expensive steaks at the Sky Crest Club.

"What's all this about?" she asked, not quite understanding what George was up to.

"That's what you used to eat when you were on the road," said George.

This was true enough. This had been her diet in her early years as a golfer.

"I just don't want you to get out of the habit," said George.

Babe ate the hamburger and the chili, and drank the buttermilk, after which she said to George, full of smiles, "I haven't had as good a meal in a long, long time."

And she meant it.

In 1951, Babe had her own golf club. This was George's

idea, too. They bought the old Forest Hill Country Club in Tampa, Florida, made some changes, some improvements, and renamed it the Tampa Golf and Country Club. Of course, Babe's presence was enough to build up the membership of that club rapidly. It proved to be a good financial investment.

But it wasn't all roses, peaches and cream, for Babe. As early as 1948, Babe was going to discover that she was not superhuman. She was to learn that even the greatest of athletes can be brought down by pain, by some inexplicable physical ailment.

It happened at an award-presentation affair for golf caddies. She was having a great time, as she always did at such affairs, with Bing Crosby, Bob Hope, Jimmy Demaret, Frank Stranahan, Patty Berg, Louise Suggs, and others, when she felt a sharp pain in her left side.

She shook it off, but on the plane, homeward bound, the pain returned, and it was severe.

Babe went into the ladies' room and examined herself. The pain was coming from a swelling on her back.

"I should see a doctor about it," she said to herself; but she didn't.

The pain went away, after a while. So did the swelling. But both returned to discomfort her.

She discovered that a hot bath and a good night's sleep seemed to ease the discomfort and bring down the swelling. While she knew that eventually she would have to consult a doctor about it, she kept putting the visit off.

"I'm too busy right now," she would say to herself. "The doctor can wait."

George Zaharias knew nothing of the situation. Neither did anyone else. Babe just didn't talk about it. She went right on with her golf chores.

In 1951, she won the Ponte Vedra Open in Florida. She was the winner at the Tampa Open, the Orlando Two-ball tournament, the Fresno Open, the Richmond Open. She also took the All-American tournament, the Texas Open and, again, the World championship.

That pain and swelling didn't seem to hamper or to slow down her game.

In 1952 it was much of the same, at the beginning. Babe led the field at the Miami Weathervane, and again at the Orlando Two-ball. She was No. 1 in the Augusta Title-holders tournament. But the pain in her left side was stronger than ever, and the swelling was more pronounced. At the Richmond Women's Open, in Richmond, California, Babe suddenly began to feel faint, and she was lucky to finish fifth in the tournament.

"Something wrong, honey?" asked George as she came off the golf course.

Babe had to tell him.

"You'd better take some time off and see a doctor," said George.

George was a worrier. He was especially a worrier when it came to Babe. Babe meant more than anything else to this big hulk of a man. He would break down and cry at even the least thought that anything might be wrong with her.

But Babe insisted that she had to go on with her tour.

She didn't do too well at her next tourney, at Bakersfield, but, despite the pain, which would not leave her now, she took the Fresno Open.

In Seattle, for the third leg of the Weathervane, Babe finally had to give up her resistance to that long-postponed but now necessary visit to a doctor.

"I think I'd better go to a hospital, George," she said.

George, tears in his eyes, said, "I think you'd better."

A plane carried them to Beaumont. There was only one doctor Babe wanted to see, Dr. W. E. Tatum, her old family doctor. And she saw him none too soon.

At the Hotel Dieu Hospital, where a room had already been reserved for her, by wire and telephone, Dr. Tatum said, very gravely, "Another week and I wouldn't have been able to do anything for you."

It was a femoral hernia already in the strangulating stage. Strangulation would have killed her.

Happily, Babe had that week. The operation she had to undergo was a complete success and, almost in no time, Babe was out of bed swinging her beloved golf clubs.

Fast as was her recovery, however, it wasn't fast enough for Babe Didrikson Zaharias. She kept calling Dr. Tatum in Beaumont, from her Tampa home where she was recuperating, asking him when she could get back to the game.

The doctor kept putting her off.

She missed the National Women's Open and the All-American. She finally was able to enter the World championship and, despite her weakness after the operation, finished third. The Babe, however, was strong enough to take the Texas Women's Open and, for a little while, she was the old Babe, sitting on top of the world.

That feeling wasn't going to last too long.

Babe took the Texas Open in October. It wasn't more than a month later that she began to again feel that something more than the hernia was wrong with her.

Eventually this something, gnawing away in some hidden spot, would cut short her brilliant career on the golf courses of the world, would cut short her life.

## Chapter 17

AT THE end of the 1952 tournament season, Babe was a very tired young woman. It had been a strenuous season. She had had the hernia operation. She might very well have expected to be tired.

What bothered Babe was that she did not snap back in her usual manner, after a short rest. Now she was always tired, no pep at all. She couldn't shake the lethargy. She was packing up her golf clubs when she should have been out on the course. It took an almost superhuman effort for her to go eighteen holes. More often, just nine holes proved more than enough for her. She was sluggish, tired, aching. And she was worried.

George, of course, was worried, too.

"Why don't you take a long rest?" he said. "Maybe we ought to take a trip somewhere? Do you think you ought to see a doctor?"

He hovered over her, protective as ever, and deeply concerned.

Actually, things hadn't gone too well between Babe and George for a considerable period of time. Babe had been off alone, on her tours, her exhibitions, and had been leaving George back home in Tampa. As George saw it, she was slipping away from him, and there were big rows about it.

Babe's friends felt she had outgrown George, that she now preferred the more genteel type of people she met at golf clubs and parties rather than the coarse, ungainly wrestlers George palled with.

There was the time when she was in New York without him and appeared as a guest on a number of television shows, collecting fees of $1,000 and $1,500 for each of her appearances. Everyone from Ed Sullivan down wanted her on their big television shows.

George didn't mind these TV appearances. He enjoyed them. What he didn't like was the fact that Babe was doing it on her own. He was afraid she would be so independent that she wouldn't be needing him.

When Babe called him, home in Tampa, to tell him she had made $6,000 for doing her turns in the TV studios, he blew up.

"I want you to come home!" he shouted into the phone. "I want you home fast."

"I'll be home!" snapped Babe. "When I'm ready to come home!"

She slammed down the telephone receiver.

She turned angrily to her best friend Betty Dodd, who was with her at the time.

"Damn!" she exploded. "If he thinks I'm going home so he can book me in some exhibition for $300, he's crazy!"

Babe's close relationship with Betty Dodd was something else that bothered George.

Betty had been sent to Babe by a very old friend of Babe's, Bertha Bowen. Betty was a young pro golfer, and Mrs. Bowen had asked Babe to look after her.

Babe and the younger Betty Dodd took to each other immediately, and for good reason. In many ways they were much alike.

Betty came from an excellent family background. Her father was a general. But Betty was all tomboy. She would rather play her guitar than comb her hair. She would rather swing at a ball than preen before a mirror. Her clothes, her whole appearance, were enough to shock the proper ladies with whom she constantly came in contact.

Babe took her in hand. They loved to play jokes on each other.

Babe would play the harmonica to Betty's guitar, at the drop of a hat, on or off the golf course. Once, when Louise Suggs was about to make a crucial putt, much to the amusement of the gallery, but much to the annoyance of Louise, Babe and Betty took out their instruments and went into one of their more boisterous performances. It wasn't that they wanted to put Louise off her game, it was the gallery they wanted to please, and they both knew how to do it.

Betty was Babe's protégée.

Babe took Betty's golf game in hand. She also worked arduously on Betty's dress and manners. She even fixed Betty's hair, giving the younger girl a permanent.

"I'm going to make a lady out of you if it kills you!" she would shout at Betty Dodd, running the comb through her unruly hair.

"She's a daughter to us," said Babe, giving George a responsibility he enjoyed less and less with time.

George didn't like this attachment between his wife and the young girl. Betty and Babe roomed together on their tours, whenever Babe was away from home. The fact is, George was plain jealous. And he made that jealousy plain to Babe.

Quarrels between Babe and George grew more frequent. The words between them grew sharper and louder. There

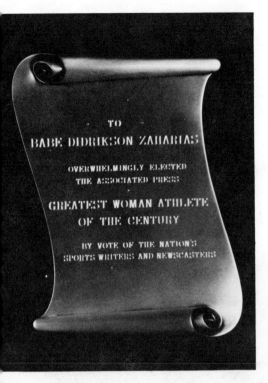

The Associated Press voted Babe Didrikson the "World's Greatest Woman Athlete of the First Half of the Twentieth Century" in 1953 and presented her with this handsome plaque.
(Photo Courtesy Joe Heiling, Sports Editor, Beaumont *Enterprise*)

Citizens of the Beaumont, Texas, area initiated a drive to establish a Babe Didrikson memorial in 1970, and with the help of a number of contributions from fans of the Babe, this beautiful museum was erected in Beaumont. The museum contains most of Babe's trophies, awards, photographs, and scrapbooks. Ben Rogers, president of the Babe Didrikson Zaharias Foundation, and Thad Johnson, secretary, guided the organization during the early stages until the museum was built. Today thousands of schoolchildren and adults visit the museum annually. (Photo Courtesy the Babe Didrikson Zaharias Memorial, Beaumont)

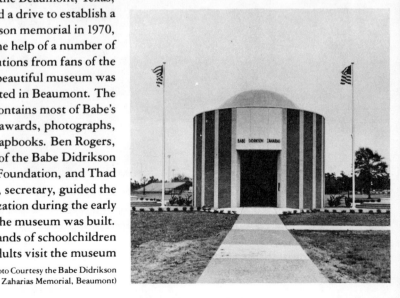

Homeward bound. George Zaharias and wife, Babe Didrikson, wave as they board a plane at New York's LaGuardia Airport, July 2, 1947, for their Denver home. The Babe returned to this country June 30 after winning the British Women's Open golf championship in Scotland. It was the first time in history that an American woman golfer had ever won this historic golf crown.

(Photo Courtesy New York *Daily News*)

Babe sets course record. Babe Didrikson takes a practice swing at Fort Smith, Arkansas, on October 16, 1947, before shooting a record 68—11 under par—to take a seven-stroke lead in the Women's Open golf tourney. Babe won the tournament three days later.

(Photo Courtesy Joe Heiling, Sports Editor, Beaumont *Enterprise*)

The champ—August 6, 1950. Babe Zaharias (Didrikson) and Patty Berg (left) check scores after the final round of the All-American Women's golf tourney as Promoter George May looks on at the Tam O'Shanter Country Club near Chicago. Babe won the championship with a record-breaking score of 296 for the seventy-two-hole route. Patty Berg finished second with a score of 306.

*(Wide World Photo)*

The Babe grins. Mildred (Babe) Didrikson Zaharias gives a satisfied grin as she reads an advance copy of the Associated Press wire story that named her 1953's outstanding woman athlete.

*(Wide World Photo)*

Babe Didrikson, considered the greatest woman athlete the world has ever known, participated in many sports. She was an All-American basketball player; a champion golfer who won more golf titles than any

other woman; she won two gold medals in the 1932 Olympics, played
an outstanding game of tennis, and even boxed with pro boxer Barney
Ross in a series of exhibitions.

The Babe makes golf history. Babe Didrikson made golf history in 1947 when she became the first American woman golfer to win the British Women's Amateur golf championship. On the Gullane course, Scotland, Babe defeated Miss Jacqueline Gordon in the thirty-six-hole final. Photo shows Babe holding the coveted trophy after the presentation by Lady Tweedle of Gifford.

were rumors of a separation between them, of divorce and, actually, Babe and George did talk about divorce.

It was an odd situation—and eventually their marriage soured to the point that Babe turned elsewhere for comfort and support.

All the quarrels, all the suspicions, all the talk of separation and divorce, however, were behind them in the winter of 1952.

Babe, obviously, wasn't well, and George, the husband who adored her, watched over her like a hawk. He had only one thing in mind: Babe had to get rest, and he did everything he could to make her life restful and peaceful. She had to get well, and he kept urging her to get the medical attention she so definitely needed.

But Babe wasn't going to be a patient, not as long as she could help it. Despite all the pleading that George could muster, she was up there at the tee in the very first tournament of the 1953 season. She was a woman of remarkable courage. It was a depth of courage that was yet to amaze the entire sports world.

It was obvious to everybody, from the very beginning of the 1953 tour, that Babe was not well. Still, she was not to be denied. If the best she could do at the Tampa Open was to come in sixth, she was second at the Miami Beach Open and at the Orlando Two-ball tournament.

At Sarasota, her strength seemed to return, and she took that Open for the first victory of the season. At the Jacksonville Open and the New Orleans Open, she managed to take second place in each tournament.

But at the Peach Blossom-Betsy Rawls tournament in Spartanburg, Babe had to use her last ounce of energy just to finish the eighteen holes, and completely out of the money.

"You just have to see a doctor!" yelled George, not in anger but in desperation.

"I'll be all right," said Babe.

She always said, "I'll be all right."

George insisted.

"You're killing yourself!" he said.

"All right, all right," said Babe.

She knew she had to see a doctor, but she pleaded for time.

"We'll be in Beaumont in a couple of weeks," she said. "I'll see Dr. Tatum for a checkup when we get there."

Beaumont had honored Babe, naming their golf tournament after her. Babe wanted to win the Babe Zaharias tournament desperately. She did, putting for a birdie on the eighteenth hole to nose out Louise Suggs, 217 to Louise's 216.

When the last hole was played, Babe barely managed to walk to the clubhouse. She didn't have the strength to pack her things after the game. The tournament had taken all but the last bit of energy out of her.

"Pack my things," she said to George, who never left her now. "I have to see Dr. Tatum. I feel awful sick."

"Go ahead," said George. It was George who had arranged the appointment with Dr. Tatum. "I'll be right there."

Dr. Tatum checked on the operation Babe had had, the year before, for that strangulated hernia.

"Looks fine," said the good doctor.

He probed around, the way doctors do, Babe keeping her eyes on him all the while to see whether she could detect some reaction on his part. What Babe saw didn't please her.

The more the doctor probed, the paler his face seemed to go.

"Anything wrong?" asked Babe.

"I'm not sure," said Dr. Tatum.

Babe looked at the doctor. She looked at him hard.

"It's cancer," said Babe. "Is that it, doctor? Cancer?"

"I wouldn't say that!"

The doctor was quick with his answer, too quick.

"What makes you think it's cancer?"

"I don't know," said Babe, thoughtfully. She really wasn't afraid. "It's just that I've suspected it for a long time now."

"Too many people suspect they have cancer," said Dr. Tatum. "Or maybe not enough."

He managed a small smile. The smile disappeared fast.

"We want to check every possibility," said the doctor. "That's all."

"Check what?" asked Babe.

"I'm not sure," said Dr. Tatum. "There's a specialist in Fort Worth. A proctologist. I want him to make some tests."

"You think I need those tests?" queried Babe, still digging for some more definite response from her doctor.

"Yes," said Dr. Tatum. "You definitely need them."

"O.K.," responded Babe, giving up on her drive for information that might be a little more specific. "I'll see him in October, after the Texas Open."

"You'll do nothing of the kind. You'll see him right away," came back Dr. Tatum. "I'm calling him right now to arrange for your appointment."

"As serious as that?" asked Babe.

"It's serious enough," said the old doctor.

"You make the appointment, Dr. Tatum," said Babe. "I'll be there."

Babe may have recalled at that unhappy moment the lines Grantland Rice had written for her almost twenty years ago.

> From the high jump of Olympic fame,
> The hurdles and the rest.
> The javelin that flashed its flame
> On by the record test—
> The Texas Babe now shifts the scene
> Where slashing drives are far,
> Where spoon shots find the distant green
> To break the back of par.

She may well have recalled those lines and wondered whether the days of the slashing drive, the great interest and excitement in her tourney play, the putting greens, would soon be over for her, forever.

When her mother had died, two years after her father's death, Babe had called Peggy Kirk Bell and Marge Row into her room. They were two of her fellow golfers on the tour, but neither one had been a particular friend of the Babe's.

Babe was playing the harmonica when the two girls came into her room.

"She didn't say anything to us," reported Peggy Kirk Bell. "She just sat there all night, as if she were in some other world, playing her harmonica. And we didn't know what to say to her."

Leaving Dr. Tatum, that afternoon in April of 1953, the Babe didn't play her harmonica.

"We have to go to Fort Worth," she said to George. "They're going to test me for cancer."

And George cried.

# Chapter 18

BABE's APPOINTMENT with noted cancer specialist Dr. William C. Tatum, no relative of the Beaumont Dr. Tatum, was for Monday, at eleven in the morning.

She and George arrived in Dallas Sunday evening. They stayed with old friends, the Bowens. Bertha Bowen was one of the women who helped run the women's golf tournaments in Texas. When Babe was having her troubles with the United States Golf Association, Bertha was one of the people who came to her defense and fought for her. She had opened her lovely home to Babe and befriended Babe at the lowest moments in her golf career.

"Come in!" she said to Babe, and to George, too, as she opened her doors for them.

She had received advance notice on what was troubling Babe. She noted George was carrying her golf clubs, and hopped on those clubs as a way of introducing some cheer into the dark and heavy atmosphere.

"I'm so glad you brought them!" she said, cheerily. "Perhaps we can play a little golf before you go back to Beaumont."

There would be no golf in Dallas—not then, and certainly not for Babe, anyway.

George had Babe down to the doctor's office at exactly eleven, the appointed hour, the next morning.

The doctor was waiting for them.

Bad news travels fast.

The newspapers had it all down in print almost before the doctor could begin to take those smears, the biopsies that would reveal the depths of Babe's ailments.

"Mrs. Zaharias, the greatest athlete in the world," wrote Paul Martin, a local sportswriter, "one of the most outstanding all-around athletes in history, was in Dallas this morning to undergo extensive tests for an ailment described as something along the line of a malignancy."

The reporters also knew, and printed, the fact that it would be "forty-eight to seventy-two hours before Dr. Tatum could make a definitive report on Babe's condition."

There would be nothing sacred or private about the ordeal that Babe Didrikson Zaharias was to suffer.

At one time Babe might have said about those newspaper reports, since she was never one to shy away from publicity, "I don't care what they write, just so they spell my name right."

That evening, at the Bowens', she did not even look at the papers.

She was worried.

The Bowens were worried.

George was worried.

Early Tuesday morning, just about twenty-four hours after their visit with Dr. Tatum, George got up from his chair, and impulsively declared, "I'm going to see the doctor!"

"What for?" asked Babe. "He said he wouldn't know anything till Wednesday."

"I just want to get checked out myself," said George. "Do you mind?"

Babe didn't mind. She didn't mind anything at that moment. "Go ahead," she said.

George got his checkup. He was O.K. But it wasn't for his checkup that he had gone to see Dr. Tatum. Babe knew that. The doctor knew that. George just couldn't sit in the Bowens' house any longer, comfortable as they made it. He just couldn't wait those forty-eight hours for the report on Babe's condition.

"Thanks, doctor," he said to Dr. Tatum. "It's good to know there's nothing wrong with me."

Then, turning sharply on the doctor, he sputtered, "But how about my wife? How about my wife, Dr. Tatum?"

The doctor didn't fence with George. The situation was too serious for that.

"I'm afraid," he said, perhaps clinically but certainly sadly, "I'm afraid your wife has cancer."

"Are you sure?" pleaded George, the tears pushing into his eyes.

The doctor nodded his head.

"I'm sure."

George bolted out of the doctor's office, tears running down his face. He didn't know where to go. He didn't know what to do. The one thing he was sure of was that he didn't want to go back to the Bowens'. He didn't want to tell Babe that she had cancer.

He walked the streets for a while, trying to compose himself. Finally he found a telephone booth and dialed the Bowens' house.

"Babe," he said, trying to lick the lump that kept coming up in his throat, "I'm going to see a couple of movies, honey.

You know how I like to see movies. Don't wait for me for dinner. I'll get something to eat somewhere downtown. See you later, honey."

Then the tears came again. He went to the movies, but he saw nothing on the screen. He sat in that movie house for more than three hours, softly crying to himself.

When he got home, Babe was in bed, but she wasn't asleep.

"Better get some sleep, honey," he advised her.

"You'd better get some sleep," said Babe, after a while.

Neither one could fall asleep, Babe worried about what the doctor was going to report, George knowing what that report would be.

They talked for a while, they got up to make some coffee in the kitchen, they said nothing of doctors, of biopsies, of that dread word, cancer.

When they finally did fall asleep, toward morning, their hands were clasped, Babe's hand in George's hand, as if each feared losing the other.

Wednesday morning, Babe and George were prompt getting down to Dr. Tatum's office.

Babe was nervous, hoping against hope that whatever the doctor had discovered, it wouldn't be cancer.

George, of course, was nervous, wondering how Babe would take the bad news he had already heard.

The doctor was mercifully direct and brief.

"Babe," he said, "you've got cancer."

For Babe, though she had long suspected the truth, the news hit her "like a thunderbolt."

That is how she described her reaction to the dreadful news she heard that morning in early April of 1953.

George reached for her hand, fighting the tears again, and held it as the doctor explained Babe's situation.

"The cancer is in the rectum," he said, clinically. "You'll need a colostomy."

There were pictures and diagrams.

"It will be necessary," the doctor went on, "to cut off part of the lower intestine to remove the cancer. The intestine will have to be rerouted and a new outlet established in the left side of the abdomen."

For a while, it was like listening to some analytical report on surgery that would have to be performed on some third person. But the truth could not be avoided for too long. Babe was crying as she left the doctor's office. And George, who had never seen Babe cry before, sobbed, his face bathed in tears.

Back with the Bowens, Bertha, distressed as she was, made a brave effort to console Babe, comfort her, instill her with some hope.

"Lots of people have colostomies," she said, as cheerfully as she might. "They get well again and they're as good as new."

Babe wouldn't be consoled.

"Here," she said to Bertha, offering her old friend her golf clubs, "I want you to have them. I won't be needing them anymore."

But before Bertha Bowen could protest, George had snatched the bag from Babe's hands.

"No, honey!" he exclaimed. "You'll be needing them! You're going to play again!"

George quickly carried those clubs out of the house and put them into the car, not because he really believed what

147

he had said about Babe's playing again, but to conceal the gush of tears that poured from his eyes.

A Fort Worth newspaper had already printed a story full of gloom and doom.

"Mrs. Zaharias has engaged in her last athletic competition," the sportswriter wrote.

Another newspaper report had it that "The further participation of Mrs. Zaharias in competitive golf is unlikely. If she does compete again, her play will not be of her usual championship caliber."

A reporter for the Texas *Star-Telegram* put it most bluntly:

"According to best medical opinions, Mrs. Zaharias will never play golf again."

How wrong these people were! The story of Babe Didrikson Zaharias' fight against cancer is one of the most heroic in the annals of any sport, or of any of the walks a man or woman takes through life.

# Chapter 19

BACK IN Beaumont, Babe was in the Hotel Dieu Hospital again. There were to be more tests and more X rays before they wheeled her to the operating table.

Neither Babe nor George had spread the news, but the newspapers did a good job of it, and everybody in the country knew that Babe was to undergo surgery for a "serious malignancy."

Wires, letters, and flowers began to pour into Babe's room at the hospital.

"You are going to be O.K.," telegrammed Walter Winchell, the New York columnist.

From the Masters tournament in Augusta, Georgia, forty sportswriters signed a wire to her.

"Best of luck and love from your sweethearts in the press box."

Lou Boudreau, Del Baker, Bill McKechnie, and the entire squad of the Boston Red Sox sent her a wire. So did the Philadelphia Phillies baseball club.

Ed Sullivan, Bobby Jones, Pepper Martin, Fred Waring, Clark Griffith, and a host of other celebrities in the sports and entertainment world wired her. So did hundreds and hundreds of others, both men and women.

Bob Hope, Mickey Rooney, and Grantland Rice, among a

myriad of others, had her on the phone. There were more than twenty thousand letters from all over the world.

So many flowers came into her room that Babe asked the nurses to distribute them to the less fortunate patients who had no flowers at all.

It was good to know that so many people were concerned about her, wishing her well, praying for her. It was good, too, to learn that the X rays revealed that the cancer was localized, that it hadn't moved to the rest of her body, but the idea of the colostomy weighed heavily on Babe's mind. It was an insult, as she saw it, an injury to her body.

Betty Dodd, trying to comfort Babe, told her that a colostomy was sometimes no more than temporary surgery, that sometimes the doctors were able to reconnect the intestine at a later date. This is what she hoped for, as the letters, the wires, and the phone calls kept coming in, and all her family and some good friends spent the long hours at her bedside in the hospital.

On the afternoon of April 17 they came to take her to the operating room.

There were kind and encouraging words from everyone around her, her family, the nurses, even the orderlies.

"Don't worry," Babe said to them. "I'll be all right. I'm leaving everything in the hands of God."

George held her hand and Betty at her side talked calmly to Babe as they wheeled her out of her room. George held her hand until they opened the door to the room where the surgeons were waiting for her.

"I'll be all right, honey," she kept reassuring her good husband. "Just you get my golf clubs and put them in the corner of my room."

She was referring to her hospital room.

"I want to look at them when I come out of the operation. I want to know that they're there. I'm going to use them again, honey. I'm going to use them."

To the reporters who were hovering in the halls around her, she said, "Tell everybody to pray double hard for me and I'll be back."

"And tell the people to send their money to the Cancer Fund instead of sending me flowers."

George bent down to give her a kiss.

"I know you're going to be all well again," he said, his voice choked with the tears he held back. "It's going to be like old times again," he said.

He kissed her once more, and Babe was wheeled into the operating arena, and the doors closed behind her.

Babe was on the operating table for four hours. George was waiting for her as they moved her out of the room.

She opened her eyes and saw him as they wheeled her to the elevators.

"I'm all right, honey," she said, and she fell asleep again.

She would sleep most of the next three days.

George saw to it that there were enough nurses for her, night and day. Betty Dodd, her protégée and closest friend, had the hospital put up a cot for herself in Babe's room. She would stay with Babe the whole time she was at the Hotel Dieu Hospital.

The first thing Babe looked for, when she finally came out of her long sleep, was her golf clubs. They were there. George had done as she asked. She kept looking at those golf clubs all the time. Right from the start, she was determined to use them again.

She looked at her lean arms and legs. She had lost a lot of weight. She needed strength in her arms and legs if she was to play golf again, so she began to exercise them, even as she lay in bed. The first time she was allowed to leave that bed, for only moments, she picked up a golf club and gripped it, gripped it as hard as she could. The grip was weak. She knew that. But she would work on that grip till the wood was firm in her hands.

Slowly, very slowly, Babe grew stronger. She began to welcome her visitors. She sat up in her bed and began to play her harmonica again, and Betty Dodd had her guitar with her, so they could make music together.

Babe recuperated quickly, more quickly than either she or the doctors had expected. Home, in Tampa, after her release from the hospital, Babe was soon out of doors, swinging her golf clubs.

"Don't you think you ought to ask the doctors about that?" asked George.

Babe called the doctors.

"Perfectly all right," said the doctors. "We thought you'd be at it a long time ago."

Babe went at it slowly but steadily. First it was one hole, then two, then nine. In almost no time at all, Babe was back on the golf course and in the tournaments. Only 3½ months after that crucial operation and the colostomy, Babe was teeing off at the Tam O'Shanter Country Club in Niles, Illinois.

There was a huge crowd, as usual, to watch her. This crowd was even larger than most.

"Can Babe come back?"

"Can she play tournament golf again?"

These were the questions in the minds and on the lips of both spectators and sportswriters.

Babe answered those questions quickly.

She stepped up to the tee and took her first swing. The ball sailed 250 yards, and it went straight down the middle.

The gallery went wild, applauding, shouting, cheering. The Babe was back!

But not so fast.

Babe was still to regain her full strength. Eighteen holes were still a little too much for her. Seventy-two holes were certainly too much for her. Still, she managed to come in fifteenth among all the women competing in the All-American that year, at the Tam O'Shanter Club.

This was surely far off her regular form, but Babe was thrilled. She knew that once she regained her full strength, despite the colostomy, she would regain the form that made her the greatest woman golfer in the world.

Two days after the All-American, she was playing in the World championship tournament. After 3½ grueling rounds, she held a lead over the entire field. All her optimism seemed to be paying off.

"Then I ran out of gas," said Babe, speaking about the tournament. "My back was killing me and it was an effort to swing my clubs. I had to sit down between shots to rest. I was tired and felt sluggish."

Both Patty Berg and Louise Suggs passed her. Babe came in third at the World championship with a 304. It was a respectable 304, and Babe was saying to herself, "Wait till next year."

She had plenty of reason to be confident.

All the reports, medical and newspaper, had predicted that Babe would no longer be able to play tournament golf. She had proved all those reports wrong.

Despite the fact that her tournament play had to be sharply cut because of her bout with cancer, the hospitalization, and the operation, she had won $6,345 on the professional golf course in 1953 and finished No. 6 in the ranks of the money-winners.

And she was awarded the coveted Ben Hogan Comeback of the Year Award, as well.

Of all the things Babe did to deserve her ranking as the greatest woman athlete of all time, there was nothing that quite approached the determination and sheer bravery she displayed during her sensational recovery from the doctor's prognosis of "never again." What Babe did not know, however, was the talk both George and Betty Dodd had with Dr. Robert Moore, her surgeon, after the operation.

"The colostomy was successful," said the doctor to George and Betty, "but I'm afraid we've found more cancer in the lymph nodes."

"What does that mean?" asked George, anxiously.

"It means," said the doctor, gravely, "that it's only a matter of time before she'll have more trouble."

"Another operation?" asked George.

"I'm afraid so," said the doctor.

"When?" asked George.

"Perhaps a year," answered the doctor; "perhaps a little longer; perhaps a little sooner.

"I don't think it would be wise to tell your wife about it," added the surgeon.

"No! No!" exploded George.

He looked at Betty, quizzically.

"No," said Betty Dodd, answering the unasked question. "I won't tell her, either."

It was a secret Betty and George would keep from Babe. But the cancer grew, silently and steadily.

Perhaps it was best that Babe did not know. If she had known, perhaps she would not have had that one more great year of golf, 1954.

# Chapter 20

FOR ALL her high hopes, Babe started the 1954 season quite poorly. In her first tournament, at the Sea Island Open, Babe couldn't do any better than finish tied for the fourteenth spot. At the Tampa Open, she managed to come in seventh. At St. Petersburg, Babe flashed some of her old form and finished her rounds tied with Beverly Hanson for first place. This required a sudden-death playoff, and Babe lost the title at the third extra hole.

She began to have doubts. For the first time since her operation, some ten months ago now, she began to wonder whether she would ever win a tournament again.

But ten months after so critical an operation is a very short time indeed, and Babe's doubts proved completely unnecessary. There was going to be more than one more tournament victory Babe could add to her illustrious record.

At the very next meeting on the tour, the Serbin Women's Open, Babe came in a winner to take the $1,200 top-money prize. She was the winner again at the Sarasota Open. She was back in form, confident and full of confidence, kidding her competitors, playing it up to the galleries who adored her.

She came in third in the next three outings, the Betsy Rawls Open, the Carrollton Open, and the New Orleans

Open. She was the runner-up in the Babe Zaharias Open, then came back to win both the National Open and the National Capital Open.

It was at about this time that President Eisenhower invited her to the White House.

To Ike's wife, Mamie, Babe was as open and as friendly as she always was with people in the limelight.

"I fixed up my bangs to look like yours," Babe said.

Mamie protested.

"But you've got such a beautiful curl in your bangs," Babe said. "I just can't get a curl, no matter how hard I try."

With the President, it was golf.

"How do you do, Mrs. Zaharias," said Ike, shaking her hand warmly.

Then he moved closer to her.

"I'll see you later," he said in a stage whisper. "I want to get some tips from you. I'm not getting much distance in some of my shots. I need some tips, Babe."

There was a lot of people who wanted tips from Babe in those days. Once more she was riding high, the greatest woman golfer in the world.

At the National Open, which was played at the Salem Country Club in Peabody, Massachusetts, Babe was purely phenomenal. She won the tournament going away—running away, actually—finishing the course 12 strokes ahead of second-place Betty Hicks. The victory margin was a record. That record has been equaled in recent play. It has never been broken.

There was one more victory for Babe in 1954, the Tam O'Shanter All-American, where the margin of her victory was 8 strokes. And there was another award: For the sixth time in her career, she was voted the Woman Athlete of the

Year citation by the Associated Press poll of sportswriters and sportscasters.

Meanwhile, George and Betty Dodd never left Babe's side. Babe's victories on the golf course were a delight to them. But the doctor's prognosis on Babe's physical condition stayed with them always.

"It's only a matter of time before she'll have more trouble. Perhaps a year; perhaps a little longer; perhaps a little sooner."

Every time Babe came home with a win, George, elated, would think that maybe the surgeon had been too pessimistic. At such times he would begin to think that perhaps the doctor's diagnosis was to be doubted, that the doctor had been wrong with his gloomy predictions.

But Babe tired too quickly, even after her victories, and George would begin to worry again. There was good reason for that worry in 1954. There was more reason for George to become deeply concerned in 1955.

Babe started that 1955 season in good form. She won the Tampa Open. She won the Serbin Diamond Golf Ball tournament. The Serbin tournament, however, was to prove to be the last golf tournament Babe Didrikson Zaharias would ever win.

In March, Dr. Tatum, the Beaumont Dr. Tatum, told Babe that she needed a rest.

"You ought to take yourself a long vacation," the doctor suggested.

George, more worried than ever, insisted she take a vacation.

Babe, realizing it was the best thing she could do for herself under the circumstances, went off with Betty Dodd, and Betty's sister Peggy, to Padre Island in the Gulf of Mexico.

Babe fished off the island. She took long walks with Betty. Babe was beginning to feel herself again, and eager for the golf course once more.

One afternoon, Betty's car got stuck in the sand. All three girls pushed and shoved and pushed again till they got the car going. The next morning Babe awakened with a terrible back pain. The pains traveled to her right leg, and there was a numbness that developed in her right foot.

For a while the pains eased, but then they came back stronger than ever, and the numbness in that right foot became more pronounced.

One doctor prescribed a routine of exercises. The exercises didn't help.

Another doctor put her in traction for almost two weeks. The traction didn't help, either.

Toward the end of June, the Babe's difficulties were diagnosed as a ruptured disc of the spinal column. Once more she was taken to the operating arena. And once again, the operation was declared a complete success.

The doctors told Babe they had successfully taken care of that ruptured disc in the spinal column. What they didn't tell her was that the cancer had affected the sciatic nerve that ran down her leg. It wasn't until the end of July that they informed her of the news she must have feared for a long time.

"We've discovered a new cancer on the right side of your sacrum," they said.

"Sacrum?" questioned Babe, suddenly numbed by this latest of disasters.

"That's the rear part of your pelvis," explained the doctors.

"Bad?" asked Babe.

"We're going to give you X-ray treatments," answered the doctors.

"How about my golf?"

"It'll be three to six months before you can play again," responded her physicians.

It was a white lie. They knew that Babe Zaharias would never play golf again, certainly not tournament golf.

For a while, Babe was in and out of the hospital for the X-ray treatments. She was the bravest of women. She began to write a series of golf articles, much of which was to appear in *The Saturday Evening Post*. She never gave up the hope that she would be playing championship golf again, and soon.

"I'm feeling good and strong," she wrote to her good friend Bertha Bowen. "I don't think it will be long before I'm playing golf again."

She did play golf again, but she was way off her form.

When friends came down to see her in Tampa, she would get out of bed and would insist that they play a round with her. But her drives were weak, and she was weak. Still, she would keep going until what little strength she had was gone from her.

About all that was left of the younger Babe Didrikson Zaharias was her good humor.

The newspapers were keeping tabs on her. There were daily reports on all her activities and particularly on the state of her health.

When Babe's friends asked her how she felt, she would answer, "I don't know. I haven't read the papers yet."

Beaumont had designated April 12, 1956, "Babe Zaharias Day." It was a well-planned affair, which was to include bands and parades and floats and the usual speeches by all the celebrities who could be mustered for the occasion. Byron Nelson, Jimmy Demaret, and Jackie Burke were among the golf luminaries who were to attend.

"Whereas Mildred (Babe) Didrikson Zaharias, a Beaumont citizen," read Mayor Elmo Beard's proclamation for the event, "has achieved worldwide renown through her athletic achievements, accomplished in the best manner of American traditions; and

"Whereas, she has brought many honors to the city by her spectacular exploits in a score of sports fields; and

"Whereas, by her perseverance in the face of adversity and her valiant battle against her own unfortunate illness, she has brought renewed hope and courage to thousands of fellow Americans; and

"Whereas, the citizens of Beaumont cherish her gallant deeds both on and off the athletic field and are justly proud to have their city known as the home of Babe; and

"Whereas, the formal dedication of the Tyrrell Park drive as Babe Zaharias Drive is to take place on April 12, 1956,

"Now, therefore, I, Elmo Beard, mayor of the city of Beaumont, do hereby proclaim April 12, 1956, as Babe Zaharias Day, and I invite the people of this city to observe the day with appropriate ceremonies."

Babe could not attend those elaborate festivities. The "appropriate ceremonies" took place without her. Betty Dodd accepted the keys to the city for Babe, and the bouquet of flowers. George cut the ribbon officially opening the drive named in Babe's honor.

President Eisenhower sent a message to the mayor of the city:

"With all participants in Beaumont's celebration this week in honor of Babe Zaharias," wrote Ike, "I join in salute to her. Please extend to her host of friends—from Texas and from throughout the country—my warm best wishes for an inspiring tribute."

It was a great day for Babe, but she witnessed none of it. She was lying in a bed all that great day, in Galveston's John Sealy Hospital, and in terrible pain.

Pain would seldom and scarcely leave her for the rest of her days.

# Chapter 21

On July 13, 1956, Babe Didrikson Zaharias was on the operating table again. The pain-carrying nerves at the base of her neck were to be cut. This would stop the agony and pain from the lower part of her body being carried to her brain.

"I must warn you," the surgeon had said, "that in some cases people who submit to this operation are never able to walk again."

"I'll take my chances," Babe had said. "If I must stay in bed, I might as well be as comfortable as I possibly can be."

As she was being wheeled once again into the operating room, she said, "I'm not worried about myself. I'm worried about George."

If anyone had ever doubted her love for her husband, there was no cause to doubt it now.

Newspapermen waited around the clock for a report on Babe's condition. The whole sports world had its eyes and ears riveted on the news from John Sealy Hospital in Galveston.

"Babe Zaharias spent a restless night and still feels discomfort after an operation to relieve cancer pains" was the hospital bulletin, as reported in the papers of July 14.

"The operation was a success from an anatomical standpoint," continued the bulletin. "She can now move her legs without the previously suffered pain."

Babe told the reporters the morning after the operation, "I'm going to make it. I can wiggle my toes."

George said, with as much happiness as he could muster, "She isn't going to be paralyzed, and that's good news."

But the cancer kept moving. It was not to be controlled.

On August 6 the surgeons operated again, this time to remove an obstruction in the lower bowel.

"It was another cancer," said Dr. Robert Moore. "Malignancies have spread through her body."

"That bad?" asked the newspapermen.

"It's that bad," said Dr. Moore.

He shook his head. It was almost that he couldn't quite believe the situation.

"That woman has the most amazing grit," he said to the reporters. "She has more personal courage than any woman I've ever known."

It was small consolation for George. He knew that this was the beginning of the end for the woman he loved so much.

"When the Babe and I first realized the score," he said, "we were both bitter. She was stronger than I am and she said, 'Let's prepare now and set our house in order.' I think she has tried to be brave, but I'm not prepared for it. Hell, how do you get ready for a thing like this after eighteen years of happy marriage? I had always hoped we would go out of this life together."

He paused for a moment, to wipe the tears from his eyes.

"That's how wonderful it's been!" he exclaimed, almost angrily.

Babe was beginning to sink.

Ben Hogan and Sam Snead, playing in the Canada Cup in London, called for a minute of silent prayer for the Babe. There were players from thirty countries who joined them in that silent supplication.

All over the country, in churches and temples of every denomination, people were saying prayers for the failing Babe Zaharias.

Her condition became grave. The once-powerful Babe Didrikson Zaharias was nothing more than skin and bones now. Her weight was down to some eighty pounds.

The family was called to her bedside.

George, when he wasn't in the room with Babe, paced the floors of the hospital corridors.

The doctor came out of Babe's room.

"How is she, doctor?" asked George, anxiously.

"It's only a matter of time now," said the doctor. "I'm sorry."

George walked quietly into the room, where Babe lay almost motionless. Her eyes were amazingly large and bright in her gaunt face.

"How are you, honey?" he asked.

"I can't talk, honey," answered Babe, in a scarcely audible whisper. "I have to conserve my strength."

George left the room. He walked far down the corridor.

"Good God!" he exclaimed, pounding the one big fist into the palm of his hand. "I didn't know until now how great she really is! The last round has begun and she knows it's the last round and she's in there giving it all she's got!"

Some few hours later, George was in Babe's room again.

Babe, who seemed to have been sleeping, opened her eyes.

"I ain't gonna die, honey," she whispered, and she closed her eyes again.

Those were her last five words.

"I ain't gonna die, honey."

She fell asleep.

Three hours later, mercifully, without waking, she was dead.

George sobbed without restraint.

"Babe never asked God for too much," he cried.

All his anguish let loose.

"When she prayed she asked him to ease everyone's pain, not just her own," he said, the tears like rivers out of his eyes.

"She just prayed for Him to let her get well," he sobbed, "and she would do the rest."

"She never wanted anything but life," said George.

Babe lost her life on the twenty-seventh of September 1956. She was forty-five years old.

George lost the wife he loved, the wife who loved him.

The world lost a great athlete. More than a great athlete, the world lost a great woman.

# Chapter 22

GEORGE ZAHARIAS had devoted eighteen years of his life to Babe. He would devote the rest of his years to her memory.

He would not do it alone, however. Too many people loved and admired Babe Didrikson Zaharias to allow her to be forgotten.

The President of the United States had a scheduled press conference the day Babe died in the Galveston hospital. He opened that conference with a simple statement that had nothing to do with the affairs of state. It was concerned with that great American athlete, Babe Didrikson Zaharias.

"Ladies and gentlemen," began President Eisenhower, "I should like to take one minute to pay a tribute to Mrs. Zaharais. Babe Didrikson. She was a woman who in her athletic career certainly won the admiration of every person in the United States, all sports people over the world."

Just four days after the death of the valiant lady, the sports pages carried the announcement of the creation of a Babe Didrikson Zaharias Trophy, to be awarded annually to the outstanding woman amateur athlete of the year.

At John Sealy Hospital in Galveston, the Babe Didrikson Zaharias Cancer Fund was established, with H. W. Paley as executive secretary.

"I want the people of the world to know," said a quiet and

thoughtful George Zaharias, "how grateful Babe and I are for their prayers during her illness. Those prayers were encouraging for her, and for me, in her long fight. I am fervent in my thanks."

In 1968, Beaumont initiated plans for an ambitious memorial for the Babe. It was to be a one-floor, cylinder-shaped brick building, eighteen to twenty feet tall, and a floor space of some two thousand square feet. The structure was to house all the trophies Babe had won, ribbons, medals, scrapbooks, golf clubs, pictures, and personal memorabilia. As envisioned, the cylindrical building would form the center of five interlocking rings, in the form of the Olympics symbol. It was estimated that it would take some six to eight years to complete the construction of the memorial.

In the fall of 1975, the Babe Didrikson Zaharias Foundation presented a black-tie affair, in commemoration.

Mrs. Gerald Ford, wife of the President of the United States, was the national honorary chairperson of the Foundation. The honorary committee of the Foundation included Senator Lloyd Bentsen, Senator John Tower, Governor Dolph Briscoe, Joe Louis, John B. Connally, Congressman Jack Brooks, and Senator D. Roy Harrington.

The occasion for the affair was the showing for the first time, the premiere showing, of the MGM-CBS-television movie entitled, simply, *Babe*.

Alex Karras, the ex-Detroit Lions star and, at the time, sports commentator with the Monday night football broadcasts on television, played the part of George Zaharias in this story of the life of Babe Didrikson. A young Canadian-born actress, Susan Clark, was cast as Babe. Both actor and actress played their roles brilliantly. The memorable evening, remembering Babe, all her victories, all the long suffering she endured in her battle against the death-dealing cancer, not an eye remained dry in the illustrious audience that had gathered to do her homage.

On November 27, 1976, almost eight years to the day after its construction was begun, the memorial to Babe Didrikson Zaharias was completed and its door opened to the general public.

Visitors have moved through that door to look at the awards that were Babe's, to remember her glorious history in almost all the fields of athletic competition, to honor her memory, in a steady stream ever since. In its first two months alone, more than five thousand men, women, and children have visited the beautiful structure dedicated to the Babe.

The Babe Didrikson Zaharias Foundation had run up a deficit of $45,000 constructing the memorial, but Ben Rogers, president of the Foundation, reports that donations to erase that deficit keep pouring in.

People will not forget Babe Zaharias. They cannot forget her.

# Appendix

## MILDRED ELLA DIDRIKSON ZAHARIAS' RECORDS

### *WORLD RECORDS*

*Baseball Throw*—272 feet, 2 inches in 1932.

*80-meter Hurdles*—11.7 seconds in 1932.

*Javelin*—133 feet, 3 inches in 1930; 139 feet, 3 inches in 1932; 143 feet, 4 inches in 1932.

*High Jump*—5 feet, 5¼ inches in 1932 (tied with Jean Shiley).

*Baseball Throw*—Won AAU-sanctioned United States championship in 1930, 1931, and 1932, all world records. Her 1932 throw was 272 feet, 2 inches.

*80-meter Hurdles*—Won 1932 Olympics with an Olympic-record time of 11.7 seconds, which stood until the next Games, in 1936. This was a world record, which stood until 1934, when broken by R. Engelhardt of Germany at 11.6 seconds.

Miss Didrikson won the AAU-sanctioned United States

event in 1931 at 12 seconds, an AAU-United States record that was not broken for eighteen years.

*Javelin*—Won 1932 Olympics with a throw of 143 feet, 4 inches, an Olympic mark that stood until the 1936 Games. Her original American mark was not broken for twenty-five years.

*High Jump*—Tied for the 1932 Olympics title with an Olympic record jump of 5 feet, 5¼ inches, with Jean Shiley. Miss Shiley was given the gold medal and Miss Didrikson was accorded the silver medal when officials ruled Babe out for the "western roll." The Olympic mark stood for sixteen years.

In earning her place on the Olympic team, the 5-foot, 7-inch, 105-pound slip of a girl had won the National Women's AAU and Olympics tryouts two weeks before the Olympics, in Dyche Stadium at Northwestern University in Evanston, Illinois, single-handedly, with 30 points.

*Broad Jump*—Won AAU-sanctioned United States championship in 1931 with a jump of 17 feet, 11½ inches. Prior to this time, only Stella Walsh had jumped farther in United States competition. Didrikson's own jump stood as highest for six years.

*Eight-pound Shot Put*—Won AAU-sanctioned United States championship in 1932 with a throw of 39 feet, 6¼ inches. Only three throws by other athletes prior to that time had been longer.

Babe failed to win points in only one event, the 100-meter dash, being edged for third place in the semifinal heat.

Even in the discus, which was not her specialty, she placed fourth for an extra point.

*She won the shot put with* 39 feet, 6¼ inches; baseball throw (for the third year in a row) with 272 feet, 2 inches; javelin with 139 feet, 3 inches; 80-meter hurdles in 12.1, and high jump with 5 feet, 3³⁄₁₆ inches (tied with Jean Shiley). In the hurdles Babe won one heat in 11.9, better than her previous accepted world record.

She placed in seven events, winning four outright and tying for first in another, for her 30 points, which won the meet.

The 1932 Olympics offered five individual events for women—javelin, discus, high jump, 80-meter hurdles, and 100-meter sprint. No athlete was allowed to enter more than three Olympic events. Babe qualified for the javelin, high jump, and 80-meter hurdles.

## GOLF RECORDS

### AMATEUR

1935—Winner, Texas State Women's championship, 2 up, in 36-hole final with Peggy Chandler.

### PRO

1940—Winner, Western Open, 5 and 4.
Winner, Texas Open, 1 up.

### AMATEUR

1944—Winner and medalist, 77.
Western Open, 7 and 5.

1945—Winner and medalist, 75
  Western Open, 4 and 2.
  Winner, Texas Open, 7 and 6.
  Runner-up, Western Amateur.


### HER 17 VICTORIES IN ROW

1946—Winner and Medalist, 73, Trans-Mississippi cham-
    pionship, 6 and 5.
  Winner, National Amateur, 10 and 9.
  Winner, All-American Open, 310.
  Winner, Texas Open, 5 and 3.
  Winner, Broadmoor Invitational, 6 and 4.


1947—Winner, Tampa (Fla.) Open, 306.
  Winner, Helen Doherty, 12 and 10.
  Winner, Palm Beach, 1 up.
  Winner, South Atlantic, 5 and 4.
  Winner, Florida East Coast, 2 and 1.
  Winner, Augusta Titleholder, 304.
  Winner, North and South, 5 and 4.
  Winner, British Amateur, 5 and 4.
  Winner, Hollywood (Fla.) Four-ball.
  Winner, Florida Mixed Two-ball.
  Winner and Medalist, 148, Celebrities championship,
    Washington, D.C.
  Winner, Broadmoor Invitational, 10 and 9.


### PRO

1948—Tied second, Augusta Titleholders tournament, 309.
  Winner, All-American tournament, 309—$1,200.

Winner, World championship, 149—$1,000.

Winner, National Open, 300—$1,200.

Runner-up, Texas Open.

Runner-up, Western Open.

Runner-up, Hardcastle Open.


1949—Runner-up, Tampa (Fla.) Open, 296—$650.

Second Pro, Augusta Titleholders tournament, 304.

Winner, Eastern Open, 219—$1,000.

Quarterfinalist, Western Open.

Winner, World championship, 301—$1,000.

Runner-up, All-American tournament, 307—$650.

Runner-up, National Open, 305—$1,000.

Semifinalist, Hardcastle Open.


1950—Third Pro, Tampa Open, 304—$650.

Winner, Augusta Titleholders tournament, 208—$700.

Winner, 144-Hole Weathervane tournament, 629—$7,450.

Runner-up, Eastern Open, 218.

Winner, Western Open, $500.

Winner, All-American championship, 296—$900.

Winner, World championship, 293—$2,000.

Winner, National Open, 291—$1,250.


1951—Winner, Ponte Vedra (Fla.) Open, 223—$750.

Winner, Tampa Open, 288—$1,000. Set 72-hole record.

Winner, Orlando Two-ball tournament, with George Bolesta.

Tied second Pro, Augusta Titleholders tournament, 312—$325.

Runner-up, Sandhills Open, 231—$500.

Winner, Fresno Open, 225—$750.

Winner, Richmond Open, 224—$750.

Tied second, Sacramento Open, 76—$137.50.

Runner-up, 144-hole Weathervane, 601. Lost to Patty
Berg, 36-hole playoff, 146–147—$2,500.

Runner-up, Eastern Open, 218—$600.

Winner, All-American tournament, 295—$1,000.

Winner, World championship, 298—$2,100.

Runner-up, Carrollton Open, 222—$500.

Third, National Open, 299—$900.

Winner, Texas Open, 8 and 7.


1952—Tied third, Jacksonville Open, 236—$275.

Runner-up, Tampa Open, 298—$750.

Winner, Miami Weathervane, 145—$750.

Winner, Orlando Two-ball with Al Besselink, 1 up—
$500.

Tied second, Sarasota Open, 73.

Winner, Augusta Titleholders, 299—$1,000.

Tied fifth, New Orleans Open, 311—$350.

Runner-up, Houston Weathervane, 143—$540.

Fifth, Richmond Open, 225—$270.

Winner, Fresno Open, 226—$1,175.

Third, World championship, 308—$1,000.

Tied sixth, Betty Jameson Open, 222—$285.

Winner, Texas Open, 7 and 6—$300.


1953—Sixth, Tampa Open, 300—$450.

Tied second, Miami Beach Open, 222—$560.

Runner-up, Orlando Two-ball teamed with George
Bolesta—$458.34.

Winner, Sarasota Open, 217—$875.

Tied second, Jacksonville Open, 216—$560.
Tied second, New Orleans Open, 231—$630.
Winner, Babe Zaharias Open, 217—$875.
Tied fifteenth, All-American Open, 329.
Third, World championship, 307—$1,000.

1954—Tied fourteenth, Sea Island Open, 246.
Seventh, Tampa Open, 316—$25.
Runner-up, St. Petersburg, 216; lost playoff—$630.
Winner, Serbin Open, 294—$1,200.
Winner, Sarasota Open, 223—$875.
Third, Augusta Titleholders, 302—$400.
Third, Betsy Rawls Open, 221—$490.
Third, Carrollton Open, 220—$490.
Third, New Orleans Open, 299—$660.
Runner-up, Babe Zaharias Open, 226—$500.
Winner, National Capital Open, 299—$1,000.
Winner, National Open, 291—$2,000.
Tied second, Inverness Four-ball, 141—$475.
Fifth, Fort Wayne Open, 223—$287.
Winner, All-American Open, 294—$1,000.
Fourth, World championship, 304—$800.
Fourth, Wichita Open, 305—$500.
Tied seventh, Ardmore Open, 312—$780.

1955—Fourth, Los Angeles Open, 226—$500.
Winner, Tampa Open, 298—$1,000.
Fourth, St. Petersburg Open, 302—$500.
Winner, Serbin Open, 310—$200. Serbin Diamond
    Golf Ball.
Ninth, Serbin Open, 310—$200.
Tied seventh, Augusta Titleholders, 306—$280.

GENE SCHOOR has been associated with sports and sports personalities since his high school days in Passaic, New Jersey. After winning a number of amateur boxing championships in New Jersey, Gene received an athletic scholarship to Miami University (Florida), where the boxing team became contenders for the national championship during the years that Gene was a member of the team. Gene captured some eighteen regional boxing championships and won his way to the final round of the 1940 Olympic tryouts as a welterweight, only to lose his post on the team due to a broken hand.

Mr. Schoor has been a teacher and boxing coach at both the University of Minnesota and City College, New York, and was also a sports commentator on radio stations WINS, WNBC, and WHN. He has produced and directed radio and television programs with Joe DiMaggio and Jack Dempsey. Currently Mr. Schoor is devoting his efforts to his writing career and has published a number of books with best-selling author Robin Moore. Mr. Schoor is also hard at work on the production of two network television programs entitled "Hollywood Salutes the World Series" and "A Television Tribute to the University of Michigan's 100 Years of Football." Both these programs were originated by Mr. Schoor. The author of forty books, Mr. Schoor has written biographies of many of the nation's greatest sports and political figures, including: *Vince Lombardi—Football's Greatest Coach; Bob Feller—Strikeout King; The Story of Yogi Berra; The Jackie Robinson Story; The Jim Thorpe Story; The Story of Willie*

*Mays; Leo Durocher; Young John Kennedy; Young Robert Kennedy; The Story of Franklin D. Roosevelt; General Douglas MacArthur; Sugar Ray Robinson; Roy Campanella; Treasury of Notre Dame Football; Treasury of Army-Navy Football,* and other books of note.

# Index

# Index

# Index